ITALY OBSERVED

ITALY OBSERVED

IN PHOTOGRAPHY AND LITERATURE

Charles Traub and Luigi Ballerini   Preface by Umberto Eco

RIZZOLI
NEW YORK

To Allan Chasanoff
ὁρατικός, ἐφορατικός, προτικός

ACKNOWLEDGMENTS
The authors gratefully acknowledge the help of the following people in the making of this book:
Paolo Barlera, Miles Barth, Lanfranco Colombo, Dino D'Agata, Martin Dickson, Gabrielle Euvino,
Nathan Felde, Barbara Godorecci, Maurizio Godorecci, Thomas Harrison, Jonathan Lipkin,
Adriana Milla, Michael Moore, Tina Morelli, Richard Pioli, Alessandra Robertazzi, Catherine Rude,
Luigi Sansone, Rosanna Staffa, and Mark Towner.

Unless otherwise noted, the photographs in this volume appear through the courtesy of the photographers. Special thanks are due the following agencies: Archive Pictures Inc., Magnum Photos Inc.,
Wayfarer Photography Inc., and Wheeler Pictures Inc.

First published in the United States of America in 1988
by Rizzoli International Publications, Inc.
597 Fifth Avenue, New York, NY 10017

Permission to quote from copyright material is listed beginning on page 237.

Library of Congress Cataloging-in-Publication Data

Ballerini, Luigi, 1940–
    Italy observed in photography and literature.
    Includes index.
    1. Italy—Description and travel—Views.   2. Italy—
Description and travel.   I. Traub, Charles, 1945–
II. Title.
DG420.B25   1988   945   88-42740
ISBN 0-8478-0996-X

Edited by Jane Fluegel
Designed by Charles Davey
Composition by David E. Seham Associates, Metuchen, New Jersey
Printed and bound in Japan by Dai Nippon, Tokyo

CONTENTS

Asking me to write a preface to this book must have been meant as a provocation. Ultimately readers expect a preface to say what the book is about, and they expect the author of the preface to make a timid attempt at evaluating (benevolently, if possible) the manner in which that is accomplished. But if he limits himself to saying that this book juxtaposes pictures taken in Italy with texts that talk about Italy, he would appear to have either nothing *interesting* to say or nothing to say at all.

I cannot deny that the photos in this book were taken in Italy—or that they were taken in such a way as to make you believe they were taken in Italy—and that they say something about Italy, at least to the extent that someone aiming a camera at point X in space and time really wants to talk about point X and not about something else. Nor could I deny under oath that the texts all have something Italian as their subject.

But in bringing together the verbal and visual texts, something uncanny has taken place. It is not that I am being diffident. Luigi Ballerini shamelessly confesses in his introduction just how maliciously the authors conspired to create a fracture, a disparity between the meaning of the visual image and the word. At times, he says—and to me this seems to be the case with Everett McCourt's picture of the Ponte Sant'Angelo in which you cannot see the Tiber—the "feeling of jubilance" of the image devastates the "mean spirited" and "stolid" observations of the writer (in this case, Herman Melville). But in the pairing on the following pages (of the text by Edith Wharton and the photos by Ruth Thorne-Thomsen), the words appear to be literally estranged from what you see, a case of providing, as Ballerini says, a "multiple choice of interactions with their visual counterpart."

Here Ballerini is explicit: this project originates in Stéphane Mallarmé's *Livre,* a scheme for a mobile work born and reborn at each new reading (today Harold Bloom's readers might evoke the anagrams of the Kabbalah's *temurah*): ideally the reader, shocked by the distance separating what is read from what is seen, will dismember the book and attempt new compositions. As I write, I wonder to what extent the binding of this volume will concede the reader this privilege.

Mallarmé never succeeded in writing the *Livre:* now Ballerini and Traub have made their own attempt at it. However, a century has gone by in the interim; poetry, music, and the figurative arts have all experimented with the adventures of ambiguity and allusion—why not try an open verbal-visual work using collage? At times the juxtaposition of word and image will seem disjointed, which reminds me of Dario Fo's contemporary Italian style of theater. The American public may not be familiar with this technique, which is inspired by the patterns of the commedia dell'arte. In a typical performance, the actor speaks and says one thing while his hands, his arms, and his face say the opposite through gesture. A character might say that he wants to move straight ahead, but his arms point behind him; or maybe he holds his arms out in front of him while his legs indicate that he wants to walk backward.

Despite these conflicting signs, one assumes that this book means to talk about Italy. But rather than fill the reader with bits of data and indisputable facts, it provokes him and stirs up questions of sense. Its arguments are inconclusive, forcing the reader to think, to imagine, to recreate his or her own image of the country—which could well be different for everyone.

There is nothing extraordinary in this approach. Poetry speaks through metaphors, symbols, and images that are incongruous at times. What did T. S. Eliot mean by "I will show you fear in a handful of dust?" Nothing that a psychologist might say about fear; and a reader looking for reliable information on how adrenaline might produce an effect would quit the game. This is meant to be a work of verbal-visual poetry, not a normal picture book with commentary explaining the subject—or rather the topic.

But at this point some interesting ideas come to mind, and although they have nothing to do with Italy, I think it is right to bring them up. I would read this book as a long poem about the topic photography. The topic, in common language and in the modern theories of textual linguistics, is that about which a text speaks. When speaking, we are not always explicit in saying what we are talking about. There are languages that have a topic-comment structure. Others use a subject-predicate structure. A language such as English uses both. For example, the sentence "John hit Mary" is constructed from a subject and a predicate. With this type of structure it is tempting to say that the topic is implicit. What is this sentence talking about? Obviously, it is about the fact that John hit Mary.

However, it is not so obvious if I think about this sentence within a wider context. The statement "John hit Mary" might conclude a debate on the problems of conjugal living. It could be the way in which I define the character of John, an aggressive and violent man. It could be the explanation I give to someone who asks me why Mary is sad today. The subject-predicate structure certainly describes facts for me, but it does not necessarily say what is being talked about.

Here is an example of a sentence with a topic-comment structure: "As for education, John prefers Bertrand Russell's ideas." The first part of the enunciation establishes the topic, that which is being talked about, and thus excludes the idea that John is talking about Russell's ideas on mathematics. The first impression of the average speaker would be that topic-comment structures may be normal in scientific discourse but not in everyday conversation, where the topic is easily identified, depending on the context. But even in everyday life we are often uncertain about the topic.

Here is a recording of a conversation between a married couple, sitting in front of the television after dinner:

He: Damp evening.
She: It was better yesterday.
He: Better? But it was raining yesterday, too!
She: I'm talking about the movie.
He: But we were talking about the weather.
She: No more than five minutes ago you told me the movie was lousy.
He: What? Then you should have said: Going back to our previous discussion, i.e., tonight's movie, yesterday's was much better.
She: Listen here, we're not in court!

To avoid these incidents, some languages adopt a topic-comment structure for even the most ordinary exchanges of communication.[1] Some Oriental languages are topic prominent and have structures like this: "Elephants (topic), their noses are long." With this kind of a sentence it is clear that the speaker is interested in the characteristics of elephants. If he or she were instead to say something like "Noses, elephants have long ones," then he or she would be talking about the characteristics of noses, human and animal.

Some impatient readers may now want to ask me what the topic of this preface is. What do elephants have to do with this book? I will soon show you. We saw that when you wish, you can always establish the topic with verbal language, even if you do not speak an essentially topic-prominent language.

And in any event you can find agreement through a polemical transaction, made up of critiques and concessions. How does a photograph establish the topic?

Here we begin to touch on many problems, all of them rather dangerous, at least from a theoretical point of view. According to common opinion, photography tells the truth, that is to say it represents things the way they are. You might distrust a painting, but a photograph doesn't lie. Now newspapers use pictures to prove that what an article talks about is true. For example, in the obituaries, where it says that Mr. X died yesterday, you might think it was a joke were there not a photograph of him. We all know that the poor guy lived and had that face, and now we know he is really dead (this argument might be fallacious to a logician but not the mass media). Furthermore, to find out what we really have in our bodies, we get an X-ray or a CAT-scan. In semiotic terms it has been said that a photograph is an index, that is, a sign causally determined by its referent, just as a paw- or footprint is shaped the way it is because the foot or paw that made it is so shaped. When the police want to find a criminal, they put up his photograph and label it WANTED. Maybe that is why so many criminals get away while so many innocents are lynched.

As a matter of fact, ignoring the naive beliefs of the man in the street, photographers and photography theorists know that photography can lie and alter reality through light, focusing, and framing. It can make ugly things look pretty and pretty things ugly. It can even be shot using an old set, or be the result of a photomontage. Still, those who know photography not as a reproduction but as an interpretation of reality would be willing to admit that, at least on the level of "literal" recognition of images, a photograph is equal to a sentence with a subject-predicate structure. The picture on my passport says: "Here is a Mr. So and So who is staring straight ahead."

But let us take a look at the first two pictures in the book: in the first, by Jean Pigozzi, a man, taken from the back, looks at a landscape; in the second, taken by David Seymour, a man with a beard, shot in profile, examines from close up the frame of a painting. We are back to "John hit Mary." The situation gets more embarrassing with the third, Elliott Erwitt's picture. What do we see? A foot (for the time being we will leave aside the question of whether it is natural or artificial; it certainly is big), and then we see a street and a facade with an arch. But how do these elements relate? The only way I can identify a subject and a predicate is in metalinguistic terms: "Looking at a close-up of a foot, you see a facade in perspective." What is the third picture narrating? If we were dealing with a topic-prominent language, it might correspond to either one of the following enunciations: (1) "The feet, behind this foot is a beautiful facade;" (2) "Facades, you can see some beautiful ones by hiding behind a foot."

And so we conclude that the third picture does not assert anything because it is difficult to attribute a topic to it. But at this point I am beginning to get suspicious of the first two. Linguist Nelson Goodman said in his time that when you are in front of an image of the male figure, you never know whether you are dealing with a picture of a man or a man picture.[2] A painter can portray Mr. X but does he intend to show us what Mr. X looks like, or what human beings look like? Images, which seem more concrete than words, are instead more compromised because they get so tangled up with the universal. It seems that the word is a highly metaphysical instrument. I say "man" and I wind up expressing a platonic ideal. But then language, with its flexibility, allows me to say "that man who was sitting to your right yesterday," and from Mankind I shift to the Individual. The images seem to represent individuals, but you never know if they are being used to express abstract concepts.

Who is the man examining the frame in the second picture? I want to say "Bernard Berenson," but maybe Ballerini and Traub chose him to represent the Critic, or Vision, or the Relationship with Art. Or how about Nearsightedness? At this point captions usually come into play in newspapers and instructional books. Even Roland Barthes said so in one of his first essays on visual semiology, long before writing about photography per se.[3] The image is vague, torn between the particular and the universal. Thus the word has to intervene to anchor it: anchor it, I would say today, to a topic.

I see a woman softly pressing a baby to her breast. It is up to me to supply the caption: "Madonna," "An Italian Mother," or "Portrait of Mary Smith." Pushy, repressive, professorial, and instructive, the word assails images and decides what they are talking about. "Here are two images, one representing the Virgin and the other a pagan goddess. They are the same in figure, color, and material. Only the title is different." Who wrote this? Ludwig Wittgenstein? No, the author of the Carolingian Books, ninth century A.D.[4]

Now let us see what is in the texts opposite the second and third pictures in chapter one. T. S. Eliot's verse does not talk about the man with the beard looking at a painting. If anything, since in terms of subject and predicate there is just one pronoun in the first person, that man is we who are reading and looking (unless it is supposed to be Eliot himself). The topic seems to be ruins. But in the picture there are no ruins, just a well-conserved painting. But is any work of art, bruised and rigidified in a museum, anything other than the fragment of a ruin, a bare synecdoche of something that has disappeared? Maybe that is what the image is talking about.

If I then move on to Nathaniel Hawthorne's text, which appears with Erwitt's photograph, I find no trace of a foot. At most I am encouraged to recognize the object in the photograph as the foot of a statue. In Hawthorne, too, I find a reference to ruins. But are his romantic ruins the same as Eliot's ruins? If in reading the two texts we could stolidly suppose so, in reading them next to the two pictures we understand the infinite polysemousness of the word "ruin." If the foot is to be construed as a ruin in the sense of a glorious fragment, the ruins of the wasteland offer much less consolation. However, the painting in the photograph paired with Eliot's verse is not a fragment.

Maybe we need to reread the verse and the picture: the painting is the fragment with which someone (the man with the beard, me, Eliot?) shores up ruins that are not archaeological. Really, it is only now that I realize how incongruous it is to shore up ruins with fragments; thus neither fragments nor ruins should be taken in the architectural sense. Every metaphor taken literally is a lie. What a curious phenomenon—Eliot's text is highly metaphorical while the photograph, at a glance, is not. Instead, the picture of the foot, because of its topic, vagueness, seems very allusive, while Hawthorne's text speaks in a literal sense of ruins.

But even as Hawthorne talks about real ruins, you realize that the ruins in the picture are also real archaeological ruins, and so Erwitt's photo loses part of its metaphoric status. And as you realize that Eliot is talking about metaphoric ruins and fragments, the picture of the man with the beard becomes suspiciously metaphorical. Does the not-very-metaphoric text to number three lower the metaphoric temperature of its photograph? Or does the high-metaphoric temperature of the text to number two raise the metaphoric temperature of its photo? Is there a semiotic law that the temperature of the text determines that of the image? Could it not happen differently? What would happen if you put Eliot's verse opposite the picture of the foot? Maybe the presence of genuine ruins in the picture would lead me to read Eliot's text literally. Would the image chill the word?

This is a preface, and who knows what would happen if now, for hundreds of pages, I were to do what you, good readers, instead are supposed to do. You should move in slow oscillation between word and image and study in which and in how many different ways these counterpoint strategies work. And you must decide when the image makes you lose the sense of the sentence and when the sentence makes you lose the sense of the image. You will read a text and think that in one way or another it has a topic. Then you will compare it to an image, which by definition does not have a topic, and you will search the text for the topic (the anchor) of the image. You will not find it, and you will realize that not even the text had a topic. Or maybe it had too many.

Ballerini and Traub's work of verbal-visual poetry aims to frustrate our stubborn search for topics and to talk about Italy in the form of a myth. As a matter of fact, as Traub concludes, "The myth exists because there can be no ultimate reality." Let us try to paraphrase that: "The myth exists because there can be no ultimate topic." I would add that it is easy to reduce a myth to its canonical meaning and then to think that you have understood the ultimate reality. But the game begins again when you comment on one myth with another. And since someone said that all myths talk about the same thing, and all of them narrate each other, then try to decide how to read the myth of Oedipus in light of the myth of the Argonauts. I think this is the game played by the authors of this book.

Perhaps now I should worry about the anxious reader who cannot follow the two authors in their fearless gymnastics of reciprocal verbal-visual frustrations and asks himself why. Is the Michelin guide not a more reliable description of Italy? I might suggest that this book, just as it appears, responds to a claim Giorgio Manganelli makes on the first page: "Until a few years ago, Italy had a face." If that face was a mask, a cliche, an image circulated by the mass media, the collection of photographs and texts offered here invites you not to recognize anything anymore, and to rethink your Italian history from scratch, even in the form of a mythic narrative. There is no definitive Italy, nor is there a single image of it, except in ethnic jokes. Furthermore, a country is an adventure, and in the spirit of adventure you must live a book that invites you to re-cognize a country.

1. See, for example, Charles N. Li and Sandra A. Thompson, "Subject and Topic: A New Typology of Language," in Charles N. Li, *Subject and Topic* (New York: Academic Press, 1976).
2. Nelson Goodman, *Languages of Art* (New York: Bobst-Merrill, 1968), p. 23.
3. Roland Barthes, "Rhétorique de l'image," *Communications* 4 (1964).
4. Umberto Eco, *Art and Beauty in the Middle Ages* (New Haven and London: Yale University Press, 1986), p. 99.

THESE PICTURES, THOSE WORDS   LUIGI BALLERINI

> The Dreams clash
>   and are shattered—
> and that I tried to make a paradiso
>   terrestre
>   —Ezra Pound

> No defeat is made up entirely of defeat—since
> the world it opens is always a place
>   formerly
>   unsuspected
>   —William Carlos Williams

This is a book of words and images, of literary texts and photographs, which Charles Traub and I have assembled in an attempt to sketch out some of the most salient features of the Italian moral landscape. The photographers and the writers represented are either American or Italian. This gives the book a very special flavor, we believe. And since it reflects our own national origins, it is a very natural thing to do. The introductions are not meant to supply the reader with a typological grid; they simply ask to be viewed as opportunities to observe some of the principles and expectations that have determined the book's profile.

Our intention has been not simply to match American pictures with Italian statements (or vice versa) nor to couple American images of Italy with American verbal expressions about Italy. Neither has it been to combine into units of meaning visual and verbal texts clicked or penned by Italians. This lack of symmetry should not be interpreted as a debunking of all rhetorical strategies, however. One might gather that the words and images had been strewn together in a haphazard fashion, but that impression will surely be dispelled if some attention is paid to the individual pairings of texts and photographs. Prior to even suggesting any immersion in the shifting waters of this operation, I would offer a word of explanation as to the specific character and provenance of the texts themselves. In the essay by Charles Traub, the reader is supplied with similar information concerning the photographs.

The great majority of the excerpts from American writings issue from an observer's experience of Italy. Many of the contributions by Italian writers also reflect explicitly upon certain aspects of Italian life, but the presence of Italy cannot be determined by vernacular allusions. It emerges instead from patterns of argumentation and stylistic strategies that could only be generated by an Italian sensibility, regardless of subject matter. Should any perplexity arise from this obvious misalignment, the editors will attempt to justify their behavior by adducing that these indirect quotations have been felt to be *as* enlightening— and perhaps *more* so—than those that focus on features indigenous to Italian culture. The possibility of catching a writer in the act of being Italian has seemed as relevant to us as that of catching him looking at Italian things. Furthermore, we would swear on the head of one of our best friends that had the subject been American culture as observed by both Italians and Americans, the scales would have tipped in a similar fashion on the American side.

There is, to be sure, a second misalignment. Here, too, we hope to dispel such apprehensions as might arise from it. Although most of the American contributions date back to the nineteenth century, to a time when Italy was being discovered by an ever-increasing number of visitors—innocently curious, knowingly condescending, or both—the Italian texts, for the most part, were written after the Second World War. Over the decades, the literature of the Grand Tour—the travelogues and diaries of the nineteenth-century American visitors William Dean Howells, Nathaniel Hawthorne, Herman Melville, Henry James, and many other inspired (or reticent) victims of the dark beauty lying at the core of the peninsular experience—had provided a legacy of perceptual models for the American observation of things Italian. Whether the notion of Italy obtained from those pages is a reflection of the disposition of the writers and their culture or a comment on the nature of the situation analyzed is a question that for the time being must remain unattended. It is far more important to come to terms with the thought that this wealth of reflections also produced ideas and created moods that many Italian observers of Italy felt had to be taken to task. They embarked on a full-fledged self-appraisal, couched in the subtly stylized form of a renewed quest for realism, in the years following the Second World War. It was a time when the nation, having watched its Roman grandeur shrivel in the tragic consummation of the Fascist rite, could begin to divest itself of institutional camouflages. The same realist persuasion that inspired postwar Italian writers and filmmakers to delve deeper and deeper into their own strongly individual experience of recent history also brought about a repudiation of cultural parochialisms, calling into question that dreamy, sensuous, childish, humorous, and in the end always disturbing image of Italy that its depiction as a smoothly organized, militarily efficient nation had not unsettled.

American observations of a realist cast are available, as well, especially from the years before the turn of the century. In 1869, for instance, Mark Twain applied his harsh moralism and truculent wit to various aspects of Italian life. Yet the distance between Twain's brand of realism and the form of it that flourished in Italian literature from the end of the Second World War to the early nineteen-sixties could not be greater. The excerpted texts of Vitaliano Brancati, Natalia Ginzburg, and Pier Paolo Pasolini (pages 136, 126, 92), to name but a few of the writers associated with the revisitation of realism, as well as of such forerunners as Matilde Serao (page 160), contain scarcely a trace of Twain's supercilious deprecation. Their correctional attitudes are never the outcome of a poorly disguised outbreak of contempt. These authors would make us savor the structure of turpitude and the enchanted history of fear, foregoing annoyance with tribal laws that impede technological efficiency.

Contrasting reports of these kinds are obviously predicated on a disparity in ethical values. While it would have been possible for us to alternate the observations of nineteenth-century Americans with those of twentieth-century Italians, a counterpointing strategy would have soured at quite an early stage into a rather boring, ultimately unfair game. In objectifying our taxonomic obsessions, we have crossed more than one line.

The case of American writer Margaret Fuller Ossoli, for example, whose mid-nineteenth-century Italian hours were filled with unprejudiced curiosity for the political reality of a country undergoing unification, is at variance with the more typical instance of Americans caught in a splendid, often bookish dream based on old expectations. From 1847 to 1849, when the Roman republic fell and the hopes of its leader, Giuseppe Mazzini, were crushed by French *chassepots*, she was a resident of Rome. Her letters to the republican leader show an understanding of the *Risorgimento* rarely encountered even among native commentators. The missives to her relatives in the United States are equally astounding, for they are filled with accurate, ever enlightening details. Furthermore, her stories in Horace Greeley's New York *Tribune* (like the one excerpted on page 116), provided her fellow countrymen with rare opportunities to take exception to their Baedekers.

In a completely different vein, the line "These fragments I have shored against my ruins," from T. S. Eliot's *The Waste Land*, figures plausibly in this book not just because of its facing a photograph of Bernard Berenson examining an Italian painting (pages 20, 21) but because of the author's immersion in Italian literature, in particular the *Divine Comedy*. As a line from Dante's poem, "poi s'ascose nel foco che gli affina,"[1] is indeed one of the fragments Eliot refers to, perhaps his contribution more appropriately belongs with those quotations we have defined as indirect, ascribing them to Italian authors.

Although such crossover examples attest to the relevance of bicultural transactions, they can scarcely be said to subvert the rigid order of counterpointing. Chances are such subversions may only come about in anomalous regions where osmosis operates without intending to attain balance. Indeed, no amount of ingenious complication will ever bring about more efficacious and fruitful *dis*-order than that which results from a third, most crucial misalignment between our American and Italian literary contributions.

In Italy, the notion of realism began to lose public confidence during the nineteen-sixties, and even more so in subsequent years.[2] What had been seen as a difference between reality and this or that image of reality began to be appreciated as nothing but the difference between simulacra. Writers became keenly aware of the jagged edge separating their intended message from the one actually sent forth by their texts. They no longer called themselves writers unless they were also "language investigators," walking the tightrope between saying and meaning. Literature became that special arena where language performs acts of restlessness (including the ultimate crime of signifying through falsehood). The tumultuous prose of Giorgio Manganelli (pages 18, 122), for example, who has forged new links between language and meaning, bespeaks a tragic muse wearing a mask of grotesque laughter. Detached from the anxious world of realistic expectations, yet fully immersed in the expectant world of new anxieties, he displays a taste for mockery that is inseparable from his sense of devotion, a reticence that is mixed with nonchalance. Above all, one is struck by his ability to bring to light the surreal soul of sophistry and banality. In the bespectacled desolation of his drama, the narrator and the obliterator are one.

In contrast with earlier times, there is today a great contraction in quantity of American literature about Italy. Although this is not necessarily the result of the increasing difficulties encountered in the process of observing (and the greater intricacy of the thing observed), it may be a sign of irritation with a culture that stubbornly refuses to interpret the role in which it has been cast. In the mid-seventies, the regressive, "heavenly" role so often assigned to the Italian experience, its representation as a device to act out an unreachable exile, continued to operate in Morris West as it had in Ernest Hemingway a few decades before and in Hawthorne over a century before that. The only difference is that the Hemingways were fewer than the Hawthornes, and the Morris Wests were fewer still (although West is actually an Australian, his attitudes toward Italy are wholly consonant with those of many American writers, and so he has been cast in the role of pinch hitter). What is of interest, however, is not so much the contraction itself as that it coincides with the dissolution of the realistic model. For two decades it had provided an alternative to the perceptual attitude through which the nineteenth century continued to exact its improbable, rather disquieting toll. To properly assess the implications of the situation, it may be worthwhile to introduce the contrasting concepts of *sameness* and *otherness*. Sameness signifies the fact of belonging to a culture, and otherness, the fact of not belonging. Of course, under not belonging one frequently detects a wish to belong again.

Morris West shows a fascination for otherness by identifying a special type,

a character out of an opera (page 174)—a type not immediately available in the writer's original culture. None of his Italian colleagues, however, would be particularly interested in testifying to the unmitigated sameness of this cultural peculiarity. Mr. West's anthropological distortion is at most marginal and certainly incommensurate with the more authentic concerns of contemporary literary reality in Italy. As opposed to Mr. West's operatic figure, Giorgio Manganelli's hero, "my friend the jester," is a creature from a kind of twilight zone (page 122). Not a projection of the writer's psyche but an instrument of his writerly pleasures, this jester is imbued with the metaphysical quality of an eidolon. His role is that of the precarious subnarrator in the hands of a storyteller who has exhausted his supply of tales and can only continue to act by pretending to blot out the very figments of his imagination. "From my own fiction I will save a jester who can tell me with colorful inexactitude about the end of the great city on that day of glory and splendor. Then I will even efface my friend the jester."

The effacement of narrative and the attempted obliteration of all the screens and thresholds through which any narration must pass are thus advanced as indirect opportunities for survival: writers of this sort of "Italian" persuasion must indeed be prepared to trade the immediately referential allures of lust, pity, fear, revenge, and other venerable topics for a frightening sense of their own inadequacy, and they must extract from this exchange the necessary conditions for the deployment of a meaningful mime.

Although the indigenous mask of *sameness*, which entails the anguish of perfection and views tragedies and disasters as the mere seraphs of an impression, as doubts capable of strategies but ultimately impervious to revolutions, can no longer be directly opposed to the foreign mask of *otherness*, which entails a fascination for the unknown, a philosophy of becoming, a taste for novelties and modifications, and identifies pathos as an essential premise for the attainment of knowledge and assimilation, the notions of sameness and otherness cannot be dispensed with, and they continue to signify as the frustrated expectations of an impure dialogue, as columns standing within a landscape of ruins.

Just as those who are spurred by the urgency of otherness are bound to consider self-displacement as a way to avert alienation and to search for the essential ground of truth in the world of experience, those who swear to the intrinsic groundlessness of discourse are forced to bring out the surprisingly varied profile of sameness and to inhabit the nightmare of its everchanging manifestations. Perhaps it is owing to the bewildering fate of this contrast, which fades out without obscuring the divergent nature of its ingredients, that a picture of a distinct Italian culture can still be painted today.

That Italian writers of a postrealist faith show a disregard for the direct analysis of their own sameness is not, however, the simple result of an urge to discontinue observance of the figurative, the traditional privilege of the narrative arts; indeed, their dissatisfaction would seem to be structural: they declare that any type of ideological thinking in which the modality and activity of representing do not coincide with the form of the representation is marred by an epistemological fallacy. Like those shades that Dante treated as solid things, the semblances that are our expressions traverse the tortuous pathways of our lives, pointing to yet another life and resting only in the dream of a god.

Meanwhile, in the distance separating the literary genre of the recordable experience from that in which "forms of representation" texture their shadowy dance, there has occurred an interesting short circuit: the Italian interest in an otherness bearing the American trademark. Even here, however, there is a significant difference between cultures. Contrary to the marked individuality of the American involvement in Italian otherness, interest in things American has spread like brushfire among Italians of all classes, and one suspects that it has been assumed unawares. The phenomenon can be explained in a variety of ways. It could be attributed to the economic and political hegemony of the United States; it may also be owing to the role played by mass communications in the dissemination of the American myth. Indeed, America has been the foremost image-producing culture of our time—a sort of stock exchange for the trading of images produced the world over. However the case may be read, Italian culture has entered a semi-emulsified state owing to its lack of clear demarcations and abandonment of self-defining principles.

It is because of this gradual homogenization that Italy bears a striking resemblance to an area of the world Umberto Eco would describe as the "Periphery of the Empire," an obscure province (of the American Empire) ruled by corrupt praefects and stolid centurions, more inclined to shortsighted profligacy than to creative administration.[3] It is difficult to overestimate the humorous poignancy of Eco's metaphor, especially in light of the Dantean image of Italy as the "Garden of the Empire" (the Holy Roman Empire), an image created to separate, with typical medieval subtlety, the central, meridian values symbolized by Ancient Rome from the shady dealings of yet another disappointing German Emperor.[4] Whether or not a solution to this centuries-old conflict can be found, your editors are unwilling to say. Perhaps a few revelations will emerge from the art and literature making up the flesh and bones of this work. Examining its features, we feel that the only ground worth treading upon is one where emotions can bloom into certainties and *actes manqués* are guarantees of the sincerity of desire.

Ashes have covered the fields; mare nostrum has flooded the city. Winds and droughts and the variously outrageous fortunes of its inhabitants have wasted the land beyond description. The periphery has drifted into wider and wider circles of discontent, and the garden has grown so wild and spotty no emperor would choose it for his seat. Yet, no matter how vague the trace, no matter how faint the scent or multilayered the palimpsest, as long as the trace or scent or script is perceivable, the temptation of joining in a deciphering pilgrimage to Italy will be irresistible. Italy, after all, is a holy land, uncannily desperate as all the lands where myths periodically regenerate are bound to be: a *sainte terre*, a place one *saunters* to.

* * *

Believing that a thin, nearly imperceptible line separates didascalic activity from redundancy, we have deliberately avoided casting the literary contributions in the role of captioning the visual messages. Mutually dependent in setting up acts of transference, the photographs and literary texts extract persuasion from their complementary diversity. As the contributions by authors Italo Calvino, Natalia Ginzburg, Washington Irving, Henry James, Mary McCarthy, Ezra Pound, Gertrude Stein, Edith Wharton, and many others cast their lot with the unpredictable photographs, they literally risk having their messages usurped. By the same token, the literature may in turn usurp the outspoken specularity of the photographs.

Admittedly, the estrangement one may bring out in the other, as well as the efficiency and richness of the encounter, is directly proportional to the willingness of each one to shed its native skin. If picture and word are to merge into a single text, each must first enact the sacred ritual of emancipation from the referential bondage under which it came into being. Emancipation, however, does not mean oblivion. It means taking possession of a difference and growing with it. Even if one of the elements does not immediately adhere to at least some part of the other, the two can be made to cohere in that area which

outgrows the boundary of the encounter and could not have come into being without it. Whereas adhesions are merely the outcome of contiguity, cohesions are brought about by linking realities that are conceptually distant and can only cooperate if admitted to a common denominator by an act of the observer's imagination.

It is relatively simple to connect the image of a bottle, let us say, and a discourse on wine. It is not so simple to unveil analogies hidden in arguments related at more than one remove. The question, then, is not one of discovering that which is there to be seen (and was there all along) but rather of inventing that which can become ineluctably visible only after someone has conceived it. One must, in other words, be willing to invest in a process of making sense rooted ultimately in a sense of making—in the sense of making sense over and above the specific sense one makes. In this rupture, symbols do not stand in for things, nor act as instances of a *species superaddita*, as containers of abstract communal values, but simply inaugurate writing as the awareness of the text. Indeed, if a text were to make itself available for the act of perfect adhesion to its verbal or visual counterpart, the result of the encounter would be nothing more than an overlap, a duplication of one incapable of becoming two.

The text in excess of the sum of its ingredients is instead unsuspectable (prior to its exceeding) and brings forth a world unfettered by re(pro)ductions.

The interplay between Gabriele Basilico's picture of two young dancers cavorting on a dance floor under a spectator's empty gaze and philosopher Antonio Gramsci's remarks on the merits of an educational system one might describe as conservative, if not altogether passé, exemplifies quite clearly the nature of such a world (pages 90, 91). Although the author's words address a definite sociological problem, in their new habitat they erode the sociological frame of reference set up by the picture while lending it an affectionate but unfathomable voice of mystery. Gramsci's statement that only through "the mechanical repetition of disciplines and methodical actions" can one acquire the diligence and even the bodily composure necessary to learn Greek and Latin confronts the gap between looking and being looked at that occupies the center of the imaged text. This proximity brings about a spell of distraction that in turn activates a peculiar process of signification: the picture's mirthful realism (its first incarnation) can no longer be entrusted with a fully pronounceable message, and the worded text, with all its scrupulous earnestness, turns into a meditation on a discourse that aims at being dialectical but hangs, instead, from a cloud of mutually exclusive propositions.

Just as the picture does not simply bear witness to a rather degraded personification of discipline, so the verbal text does not exclusively reflect on the formative role of discipline permeated by humanistic ideals. What could not be obtained through mere reverberation can thus be arrived at by transcending that referential immediacy which, on the surface, seems to be the only plausible justification for the encounter of picture and words. The excess in which the encounter finds its realization becomes consubstantial with the activity of questing, with the unrenounceable despair, textual as well as psychological, that lies at the core even of the most sophisticated hermeneutical feat.

Further exemplifying this mood of recontextualizing demands is the encounter between another Basilico picture, portraying a fully costumed tenor (or is he a baritone? a bass?) standing before the toilets of an opera house, and Morris West's astonishing notion (alluded to before) that although Italian history is frequently perceived in terms of operatic grandeur, in truth operatic grandeur is but a pale shadow of Italian history (pages 174, 175). Let us compare this encounter with the pairing of Uliano Lucas's picture of a Neapolitan alley where a luxury automobile stands trapped, marked by signs of utter dejection, and Ennio Flaiano's reflections on miracles, the reliability of which, the author maintains, is commonly held by Southern Italians (pages 188, 189).

The two images differ in terms of simple photographic strategy: the former, quite obviously, has been set up; the latter has the persuasive look of a true apparition. They are also under the influence, so to speak, of profoundly divergent verbal statements. Although in the first case picture and words are topically related (the world of opera figures in both, no matter how different their messages may be), in the second the encounter is brought about by a highly plausible yet utterly pressed relationship. The first encounter has the consummate inevitability of slapstick comedy, and the second exudes the joyful candor and buffoonery of a mystery play. Had Basilico also equated Italian history and opera, or had Flaiano identified the discord between stage (alley) and performance (automobile) as a prerequisite for a miracle, there would have been no room for fruitful equivocation and, consequently, no opportunity for those instigations that flow over the one-to-one relationship of the verbal and iconic elements in the unified text. As it is, the conspicuous presence of the latrines in the first picture and the intimation in the second prose excerpt that miracles occur according to schedules more regular and precise than those governing public means of transportation deflect, more or less sensibly, and reorient, more or less skillfully, the signifying power of the accompanying texts.

Such deflections and reorientations do not presuppose any sort of genetic fault in the fabric of each element, nor, consequently, invite any attempt to obfuscate such a fault by forcing the elements on one another. On the contrary, each verbo-iconic unit is galvanized not so much by referential obligation (to Italy, of course), as by a logic and a rhythm predicated exclusively on style. It is the quality of the rhetorical strategy, the flair and flavor of the individual pictures and statements, that marks the differing motivations at the root of each encounter.

Take, for instance, Everett McCourt's picture of an angel on the bridge leading to the Castel Sant' Angelo; the photograph is paired with an entry from Herman Melville's diary, where the writer recalls that the alluvial freshness of the Tiber, despite its proximity to ancient monuments, reminds him of the primeval quality of the Ohio River (pages 216, 217). First of all, the river is nearly invisible in the picture. In fact the photo is cropped in such a way that even the identification of the bridge proves difficult. In the end, these matters of content are of no particular interest. The relevance of the encounter issues from the contrast between the angel's stately presence, which exudes a feeling of jubilance, and the rather mean-spirited, if not altogether stolid, observations of one of Rome's most famous visitors.

In contrast, a harmonious levity underlies David Hyman's picture of two worn-out chairs leaning against a table in an untrimmed garden and Luciano Bianciardi's dialogue between a lover who is curious about the partner's "first time" and the partner, who affirms not to remember at all (pages 228, 229). Here, as elsewhere, iconic interference does not result in the violation of a secret. It does, however, increase awareness of the symbolism at work in the verbal text. Although the literature has, by and large, been chosen after the photographs, and some of the quotations may have been inspired by the metaphorical qualities of the image—or by the sheer beauty of a print—the verbal texts generally tend to provide a multiple choice of interactions with their visual counterparts while leaving options open on which will ultimately be preferred.

Besides the modes of contrast and affinity, which prevail in the last two examples, parody is the pattern for a good many other encounters. Parody and encounter may indeed be perceived as contradictory terms; insofar as the former is applied to a text running parallel to another that has served as instigation, they certainly are separate, if not contradictory. Parallelism, however,

need not be rectilinear. In disco dancing, for example, the dancers' bodies do not touch but trace imaginary lines that continually cross and recross. Similarly, two texts can form a web of allusions subsuming both attraction and repulsion, affinity and contrast. Parody, then, is an equivocal mode of encounter in which the reader experiences the vagabond pleasure of a musical fugue and, at the same time, the allure of the quest for precision.

In the interfacing of Olivo Barbieri's picture of an ordinary house and the harrowing candor of Umberto Saba's poem, "The house is ruined / the house is ravaged / Arabian Nights no longer live in it" (pages 108, 109), the parodic fabric is articulated on several levels, ranging from sheer irony to melancholy to utter despondency. True parody translates such moods and passions into a "moveable feast" that lurks in every turn and every spasm of the verbo-visual unit.

These are a few exemplary events that occur when the verbal form of one message is made to react to the visual form of another. These encounters are the building blocks with which this book is constructed. The reader need not be supinely confined to these combinations, however. On the contrary, by adopting other typological axioms (such as theme, style, or social message), he can pursue a wide range of interactions within the book's present structure. Photographs can be joined with other photographs, and specimens of prose and poetry may be made to convene around a single pole; a single photograph may suit the company of excerpts assigned to other photographs, and similarly, a certain text may be illuminated by more than one photograph. Once this mechanism is set in gear, there is scarcely a way to bring it to a halt. Nor is there a desire to do so. A thorough exploration of the book will bring to light clusters and strings of significations in the same fashion that the explorations of a gold field will unearth well-defined fissures filled with golden ore.

The veins are so numerous and so labyrinthine that we have at times been "despairing of the port," toying with the idea of producing a set of unbound sheets—not unlike the project of Stéphane Mallarmé's *Livre*[5]—which could be arranged and rearranged in ever-changing combinations. In the end, however, we have succumbed to another temptation: hoping to do justice to the autonomy of the signifying process and to the referential values of the verbo-iconic material at our disposal, we have inscribed the latter into a kind of soft narrative structure, a poem, perhaps, divided into six cantos. Each is charged with the task of unfolding the style of a grammar within which *order* and *adornment* are not merely conterminous but indeed consubstantial.

In fact, while other societies may have been determined to uphold the difference between "that which is" and "that which simply appears," the Italians seem to have turned into an art of living some of the implications inherent in the relationship between cosmos (*kosmos*) and cosmetics (*kosmesis*), established by the ancient Greek tribes: cosmos, that which has order (the universe), exists and can only be perceived as the result of cosmetics, an essentializing adornment. Far from denoting a world of forgery, of made-up appearances waging a pitched battle against a true world of realities, cosmetics, like its close relative, fashion (in turn derived from *facere*, the Latin word for making), points to a sphere of experience where the perception of how something looks both precedes and coincides with the certification that something is. The seeming paradox can perhaps be explained by means of another linguistic analogy: in Greek, the aorist form of the verb for seeing, εἶδον (I saw once and for all), coincides with οἶδα, a form of the verb for knowing, which would indicate a perfect tense (I have known), were it not for the fact that its meaning is situated in the present (I know now). This means that the precedence of seeing over knowing and, conversely, the delay of knowing over seeing are formally born out of a single decision.

This coexistence of past and present in the continuity of the form may well be the most salient feature of all that can honestly be labeled Italian. An appropriate emblem for this coexistence may be the image of the seesaw, both in terms of the playfulness evoked by the object and of the extraordinary resonance of the word itself, especially when its components are appreciated (rather impertinently, to be sure) not as duplicated forms of "saw" (from the action of sawing), which they undoubtedly are, but as a staccato sequence in the paradigm of the verb for seeing (which it is not). Furthermore, the seesaw is a particularly good metaphor for the dynamics of this book: the alternation betweeen the nineteenth and twentieth centuries, the shifts between the word and image, and above all, the ebb and flow between Italian and American viewpoints.

* * *

We would like to offer one more vagabond thought on the issue of points of view. That America was chosen to provide the external perspective on Italy can doubtless be ascribed to the origins and the cultural interests of those who nurtured this book; yet it may not be wide of the mark to suppose that American reflections on Italy would be of interest beyond these perfunctory motivations. Furthermore, from some of the messages regarding Italy one might infer much that has a bearing on the image Americans have of themselves. One might also test the disturbing compatibility of messages that, with regard to Italy, have an epiphanic value, and, with regard to America, can be viewed as more or less farsighted anticipations of its future. "Whatever beauty there may be in a Roman ruin," wrote Nathaniel Hawthorne, "is the remnant of what was beautiful originally, whereas an English ruin is more beautiful often in its decay than even it was in its primal strength. If we ever build such noble structures as these Roman ones, we can have just as good ruins, after two thousand years, in the United States."[6]

Not being blessed with divinatory powers, we cannot say whether Hawthorne's wishes will be fulfilled. Nevertheless we should like to indulge our propensity for perusing a text with magnifying glasses. We note with interest that Hawthorne entrusts "noble structures" with the task of producing "good ruins." A more commonly held opinion would seem to be that far from aspiring to become ruins, noble structures would prefer to challenge time's ruinous effects. Assuming that art aims at building perennial monuments, and that literary monuments may be more durable than bronze (as Horace would have us believe),[7] one would assert that noble structures become good ruins against the intentions of their builders and that their ability to last any length of time gives testimony to the architectural principle operating within them. The stronger this principle, the longer its tangible manifestations will persist.

In the Horatian perspective, the architectural principle refuses to be confused with the destiny of its incarnations; neither is it to be disposed of as a mere trace, a deteriorated reality providing history with a kind of mnemonic support. Indeed, architecture and history can either be at odds or they can coincide. We should like to identify the former position with Italy and the latter with America. In Italy the notion of the present is predicated upon an architectural principle that burrows into its own layered archaeology and feigns imitation as a device to distinguish itself from its own matrix. A case in point is that of Renaissance Florence, Rome, and Urbino, where the imitation of classical antiquity produced a type of culture that had little to do with the model they purported to imitate.

In America, the notion of the present acquires specific meaning only if it produces images of itself that admit to no antecedent; the present becomes, in fact, particularly significant when it bestows the status of reality upon what would normally be viewed as a mere fabric of special effects. This sense of production keeps the American present from growing old. Only names pretend, occasionally, to obtain the past. Thus the Madison Square Garden in New York has since 1890 lived in three different structures, neither of the last two even located on Madison Square.

Nothing diverges more from this ever-youthful present than the Italian coexistence of past and present in the continuity of the form. What exists in the American present is the original form of the present itself (a form that continues intact until it dies), not the form in which the present becomes past and out of which it becomes present again. The American present ceases to be present when it ceases to be profitable: at that point its form is, even against all evidence, obliterated. The past is either present or it is not at all.

Caught in this divergence, Hawthorne's mode of thinking may not be logical but it is certainly heroic. Experiencing the lack of a past as a state of disinheritance, the writer not only suggests that nothing is meaningful except in its relation to history, but he goes so far as to postulate that whereas history is inferred from documents, the making of good documents will secure a good history. A devotee of echoes, he surrenders to the sirens of former splendors (and it is the sweetest of all surrenders) in the hope of contracting an equally splendid future. By striving to adopt a "European solution," however, and by doing so with more enthusiasm than would most Europeans, the writer forfeits the privilege of bringing to fruition the compelling force of the continuous present that makes itself available in America. The dilemma is then to decide whether Hawthorne's position is that of one who falls between two stools or of one who proves that a gentleman's fatherland is always his exile.

Notes

1. "Then in the fire that refines he hid," from Dante, *Purg.* XXVI, 148. As the characters in the *Divine Comedy* hid behind the fire that refined them, so Eliot hides behind the fragments that refine him.

2. In 1961, the poet and filmmaker Pier Paolo Pasolini vigorously protested the continued relevance of realism in a long, essayistic poem *In morte del realismo* ("On the Death of Realism"). Paraphrasing the funeral oration in Shakespeare's *Julius Caesar* (the dead body of Caesar becomes the dead body of realism), Pasolini addresses his Roman countrymen (the readership), stunned by the murder of the only adequate ruler (the realistic style) that Rome (Italian literature) has had. The novelist Carlo Cassola (1917–1987), a former realist who had become a reborn Belle-Lettrist, is cast in the role of Brutus ("and Cassola is an honorable man"). His faction, however, never succeeded in instituting a meaningful cooperation between literature and the cultural exigencies of the time, and could not seriously be identified as the enemy. To carry Pasolini's analogy even further, I would say that just as history did not go the way of Brutus, who after all was defeated (and committed suicide) at Philippi, so Italian literature did not go the way of Cassola. Indeed, it did not go the way of realism, either. A slow but persistent erosion was unsettling the very foundations of all the Marxist and structuralist guarantees upon which the realistic carpet had been laid. Teleological linearity was fast being replaced by hermeneutic exploration, which posited as arbitrary any form of thought grounded on previously assumed sets of values. In the end, Pasolini became more sensitive to the call of the new problematics—and in many ways tried to end a deadlock he himself had helped to create.

3. Umberto Eco, *Dalla periferia dell'impero* (Milan: Bompiani, 1977).

4. Dante, *Purg.* VI, 105.

5. In part, the memory of Symbolist poet Stéphane Mallarmé's *Le Livre* may be regarded as the inspiration for this book. According to Jean Pierre Richard, in *L'Univers imaginaire de Mallarmé* (Paris: Editions du Seuil, 1961), 565, "the central idea of the project consists of a series of public readings addressed to a small audience. The reader, or rather, the operator, must utilize a fixed number of pages and from reading to reading, take each time the same pages, but in a different order. Each new disposition would provoke the appearance of a new sense, and when one would have followed all the possible arrangements, the reader would have found himself in possession of a total, or absolute, signification."

6. Nathaniel Hawthorne, *Notes of Travel* (Cambridge, Massachusetts: Riverside Books, 1889).

7. "Exegi monumentum aere perennius / regalique situ pyramidum altius," *Carminum Liber* III, xxx, 102.

MEANING AND THE EDITING PROCESS *CHARLES TRAUB*

The story of this book's development will shed some light on its meaning and on how the photographs were selected. In the beginning was the image and not the word. Over the years I had been intrigued by a number of fine photographs made in Italy by various American and Italian photographers. They were professionals who had worked at length as serious artists in Italy. On the whole they separated themselves from the multitude of lay people who use the camera by an intent to record images that interpret rather than mimic experience. This decision to interpret carries with it a number of qualifications that constitute professionalism. Such image-makers would be disposed to look to historical antecedents, either through study of the history of photography or by a review of contemporary currents in the medium as displayed in magazines, books, and exhibitions. Professional photographers are sufficiently competent technically to take an aberration or accident and make of it a stylistic motif. Having noted a personal distinction in their work, they have developed an egocentric preoccupation with its development. And they have received outside recognition by way of publication, exhibition, or monetary recompense.

The image produced by the professional is the result not of a casual encounter but rather of the coming together of information and experience. Inherent in such a photograph is the intent to communicate specific values and to manipulate the sympathies of the viewer toward those values. It is no accident that Franco Zecchin's document of a murdered Sicilian gangster (page 157) provokes reactions of shock and revulsion and that the multilayered tonalities and precise details of Emmet Gowin's Tuscan landscape (page 235) leave one with a feeling for the sublime gentility of the Italian countryside. There is a certain kind of intelligence at work in the well-made photograph. This intelligence is communicated through a set of properties, inherent in the medium, which include tone, color, contrast, detail, scale, and composition. They constitute a vocabulary that telegraphs visual impulses and reactions that are not consignable to words nor comparable to values solely denoted by language. With all these notions in mind, I began to make a compilation of photographs that would present the cultural milieu of present-day Italy in as fair and as interpretive a manner as possible.

Many a photography book about a country has been made to document a text. Or else it has been designed to be an illustrated Baedeker, meant to guide the readers to specific sites. At one extreme is the glossy coffee-table book, luxurious in its Technicolor reproductions of scenes taken from the most advantageous, pictorial point of view, a cliché of bookstore windows of the world's most expensive byways. A volume on the wooded Adirondacks is essentially indistinguishable from one depicting the jungles of the Amazon. At the other extreme is the one-person's-eye view of a locus—usually attesting to a unique style of seeing rather than to the importance of place. Note Paul Strand's sociological stance in *Un Paese* (1954) and his other monographs on places and Robert Frank's existential alienation in his classic, *Les Américains* (1958). Though some significant welds of the extremes exist, these rarities gain their genius through a singular, unrelenting insistence upon a point of view.

Both pictorial approaches stirred in me memories from my own study of the Italian phenomenon. I wanted to create a volume of traces that would help me to regain those memories and feelings originally experienced in my own passage to Italy. In the beginning, I imagined a volume that would stand on photography alone. It would be a gathering of remarkable interpretations and archetypal renderings that would evoke memories of Italy. There would be no generic im-

ages, no sociological typologies, no "work photographs," no major monuments. Initially, no ideology was consciously present. From what was collected, the "idea" would be deduced. No structure could be imposed on photographs that had not yet been assembled. In the conventional editing of a collection of photographs, a statement is made and then supported by images. The word comes first. Here, the confluence of images in itself would provoke and produce its own synergistic meaning, which would decipher Italy or perhaps would itself need further decoding. Significance would be found in the process of seeing and in making the junctures between the pictures.

My selections would be based on a long history of experience with the photography medium, a developed eye for the mature image, and an attraction to pictures that stirred my instinctual memories of what Italy looked like. To discuss what "looking like Italy" is all about is again to sublimate visual language and adjudicate the purpose of the photographs in this book. Perhaps my definition of a good photograph will help to clarify the selection process. I hold that a good photograph is a singular and stunning apparition of something real, plausibly real, or found in the tangible world of reality. The image uses the vocabulary of the medium in such a way that the experience of the photograph cannot be supplanted by another visual medium. It is a contemplative instant infinitely held in time. A photograph looks like a photograph; that is to say, it attempts to render a scene on a piece of two-dimensional, light-sensitive paper. By means of a unique composition or vantage point, it reveals the author's intention to show that something has been created, not just "taken" (this perhaps constitutes the difference between an amateur's snapshot and a candid picture made by a professional). The photograph hints in its construction at the possibility of being repeated or of evolving in still another making by using the same or a similar set (or sets) of elements—hence, at the development of a style or peculiarity that can be mimicked but not duplicated. Photographs of this caliber reflect a felt experience that refers more to the subject than to other images made before it (except perhaps for others by the same maker). Such photographs are not clichés and do not play to preconceived views. Within the frame of these photographs, elements are placed in a balance of tensions that addresses equally what is not within the frame as well as that which is. No answers are given. New questions are raised.

* * *

Since each photograph was to be chosen not only on its own merits but also as part of a strong "collective memory" of this editor, some discussion of his disposition may be in order. I am not an Italian, nor am I of Italian descent. I have never lived in Italy, nor do I speak the language. I am frequently a visitor in Italy. I go there not out of obligation but out of desire—my travel is an act of belief. I am an alien who brings with him expectations of new delights.

Like most professional photographers, I have embarked on an occasional Grand Tour with the express desire of compiling a photographic testament to the country at hand—and to what stimulated me visually. My selection of photographs for the book was to be based on the same intention. I began by examining the work of other Americans and found that the prevailing spirit is one of empathy. Although our photographs may be laced with humor, irony, and even absurdity (witness the example by Mitch Epstein on page 75), they are without alienation and condemnation. "The Wonders of Italy" continue to be manifest in them (although admittedly the focus on the grand monuments and antiquities is sometimes skewed). Our sense of wonder results instead from an acute recognition that preserved styles coexist with twentieth-century industrial life on the peninsula. Still, the usual cynicism of the contemporary American artist has been transformed into humor; overall, Italy is viewed as an "enchanted land"—the host is respected! A clear consensus of attitudes began to emerge in making a collection of American photographs, and it contributed to one of the dichotomies that would structure this volume.

The accumulated mythology surrounding Italian culture has enveloped us foreigners like a gossamer veil. We tend to disregard the rough textures of life and follow the remnant glow of a legacy that is more seductive than the immediate disharmonies encountered en route. Myth holds great allure for one disposed to the pleasures of travel. But the allure is counterbalanced by the facts giving base to the myth. Myth is the legacy of a culture that enables the people to transcend life's adversities, and to understand it, the antecedent ebb and flow of history must be examined. Things base and real exist in all societies needing to be rationalized.

Upon turning to Italian photographers, I learned that the documentary tradition of photography is still very strong in Italy, as it is throughout Europe. There is a repeated emphasis on the sterility of postmodern life. The exploration of existential, banal subject matter is a profound motif in the work of many contemporary photographers (note the images by Mimmo Jodice and Gabriele Basilico on pages 120–121 and 145). Renowned ancient landscapes, rural and urban alike, are seen as hard, surreal panoramas rather than as picturesque pastiches of color and rusticity. Technical virtuosity often takes a back seat to intimate seeing and spontaneous, confrontational points of view. Harsh, moody tonalities dominate in color and black-and-white photographs alike.

Since it is a tendency of human beings to judge ourselves more harshly than others do, it is not difficult to understand why the Italian views his native land more critically than does the American. The resident tempers idealism with realism, for fear that he might be all the more disappointed with the facts of existence if he overglorifies them in his imagination. When the Italian conceptualizes imagery of his environment, he does so in a fashion that underlines the incongruities of the social landscape. By the confirmation of a rawer existence, he remains the artist, recreating the substance of which myths are made. As a philosopher named R. G. Collingwood put it: "If we are to be true aestheticians and concerned with the understanding of culture through our art, we cannot be concerned merely with dateless realities lodged in a metaphysical heaven but with the facts of place and time."

A dichotomy began to emerge within the collected body of photographs among both Italians and Americans, and a thesis for this project also emerged: it became clear that in the visual appraisal of a living culture, there exists both a romantic view and an opposing, coequal, pragmatic one. At the project's inception, I had supposed, too simply, that a line could be drawn between the photographic views of the American and the Italian practitioners, with the former falling on the side of idealism and the latter on the side of realism.

This packaging raised many questions that required more research than simply rummaging through photographic archives. For example, is the American, by virtue of being a stranger, inclined only to the romantic view of a land not his own? And, if so, how does he become so? What transcultural messages are sent prior to the traveler's departure and how are they transported and transformed? And, on the other shore, is the Italian self-view bound by a cultural legacy that historically values pragmatism over romanticism? What are the cultural antecedents of these views? Are the answers to these questions more readily accessible in literature? It was necessary to pursue these questions in order to give my visual discourse a supporting logic.

Thus I came back to the word. Photographs can stand as symbols, as visual impulses, but if a theme of a dialectical nature is wanted, a structure that can be cognitized and decoded must be provided. Pictorial integrity demanded more than supplying simple captions for the images. I felt that the most appropriate companions to photographs of an expressive nature were writings made in the same way. Perhaps the great literature of Italy would provide a fair parallel to this thesis, which would compliment rather than illustrate, yet add to the experience of the photographs in such a way that a more holistic image could be achieved.

It was then that Luigi Ballerini was invited to join the project. As a distinguished professor of Italian literature and as a translator of American classics into Italian, he was in a particularly advantageous position to survey both Italian and American writings about Italy to see if similar themes and points of view would emerge. Because of his broad knowledge and exhaustive research, he uncovered a multitude of excerpts, fragments, and passages that, when compared to the photographs, produced a more exciting view of the original thesis. Ballerini's choices helped to forge a strong alloy of collective meanings that would further influence the development of the project.

We reasoned that the foreigner (in this case, the American) gained a kind of romantic conditioning for travel in foreign places through reading the adventure literature of the nineteenth century. The coming of the industrial age had produced a middle class with the inclination and the time and money for journeys abroad. Travel accounts were often the first serious reading of children in the nineteenth and twentieth centuries alike. Reminiscences of the Grand Tour were not uncommon among people of means. Today's remnant of this journey exists in the American college student's summer abroad. This exodus to a distant place, the last sojourn before assuming the responsibilities of adult life, produces photographic memories that are perhaps at the root of lifelong wanderlust.

According to Ballerini, in the past century Italian literature has made its most lasting impression in the development of neorealism, which emerged following the Second World War. Generations of young Italians of the forties and fifties, unlike their American counterparts, experienced the coarse realities of war, occupation, and the accompanying decline in wealth and political stability, which left little sentiment for the idyllic.

The bicultural split between realism and romanticism was ever present in the minds of Ballerini and myself as we paired words and images. But the word-picture combinations were the results of a mutual feeling of the "rightness" of one element for the other. The single photograph no longer referred to the ethnic ideology from which it had sprung. Coexistent with its written partner, it addressed a cognizance outside its original making. The months spent in reading, comparing, and musing over the numerous fragments of literature Ballerini uncovered changed my understanding of the images previously chosen. The logic of the joining of photograph and literature grew out of a process that suited our individual understandings and perceptions of Italy. Neither word nor picture would illustrate its mate but rather make a correspondence that would bring forth a perception not apparent in either medium separately. Synergy took place with the most unlikely of pairings. It was no longer important that realistic writing accompany an image derived from the same impulse. The nineteenth-century romantic quote joined with the realism of a twentieth-century photograph provoked a more complete Gestalt of Italy than we jointly held.

Moreover, we discovered that the break between American romanticism and Italian realism that forms the underpinning of this project does not take into account the notable exceptions and crossovers that are apparent in contemporary writing and photography. The heightened speed with which contemporary Western thought travels forces ethnocentrism to take a back seat to the

THE MASK OF ITALY

Until a few years ago, Italy had a face. It was splendid and casual, and those unmistakable features fascinated Europe and all the world. Perhaps it was a mask and thus looked wiser, more allusive, more elaborate and fake—even more seductive—than any face. It exhibited a sanguine, archaic profile, with wrinkles that suggested malicious old age and laughter; it harbored signs of merry, unforgotten—vividly remembered—passions; the big mouth blended the traits of comedy and tragedy, southern brawls, melodramatic laments, puppet fights, and Punchlike loves. It was a fake mask, a collage of stereotypes and falsifications, but one so old and so awkwardly recognizable as to have acquired a certain dignity, the consumed and ruffian grace of a public image somewhere between equivocation and heraldry. But Italy was not only that vulgar and colorful image: it was also a privileged place, populated by precious, proud, and incredibly exhibitionistic civilizations given to splintered and blinding display. For two centuries, Europeans who wrote, painted, and played music—or simply read, observed, and listened—fell in love with one or another of the sacred spots in Italy: one person would lose himself in the soft labyrinth of Venice, so gothic and carnivalesque; others would embark on pilgrimages to one or another of the many Romes, all crowded, wrote Defoe (who had never been there), "with nobles, servants, and priests"; others were shipwrecked in a chaotically dramatic, nocturnal and illegal city, the catholic, baronial, dionysiac Naples; and exact and refined Tuscany forever captured Nordics desiring the sun and geometrical proportion. And yet Italy was never viewed as a peninsular parking lot full of monuments; not only were the grand objects of Italian civilization dense with intensely suggestive memories of life, they were uniquely livable, inhabitable and inhabited. This grafting of the recent onto the ancient, this biological stratification of an uninterrupted life, unaware of its impure grandeur, offered a fascinating and disturbing spectacle in which death was always ready to mime the motions and gestures of life. The secret of the mask may have been this: it concealed a dramatic, impure blending of styles, what I would call diachronic adultery, centuries of malicious complicity between the instincts and the intelligence. And so for generations impatient poets abandoned progressive, morally unobjectionable countries to live and die in this Italy of dubious morality, harassed by its decorative and reactionary grand dukes, attracted by a wrinkled and polychromatic mask, perhaps made of plaster, perhaps of flesh and blood. Does this prestigious face, this hypnotic allegory still exist? One has the impression that after Rome became Piedmontese, and from then on in an ever-accelerating rush, Italy has been lacerating that ancient body and that face with its own hands. From a gloomy Italy of supermarkets there grows around and within those genial members a mold of plastic, of seeming life. The graceful Italy is becoming a pedantic museum, with Giotto's Bell Tower connected by a wall of air to the Colosseum and the Bridge of Sighs, an Italy to inspect through catalogues, asterisks, and tombstones. Or does the keen, more loving eye of the foreigner, the heir of Shelley, Goethe, and Stendhal, still know how to distinguish the ruins from the scraps, a fragment of the mask, the wisdom of a wrinkle?

Giorgio Manganelli, 1973

Photograph: Jean Pigozzi. *Florence*, 1978

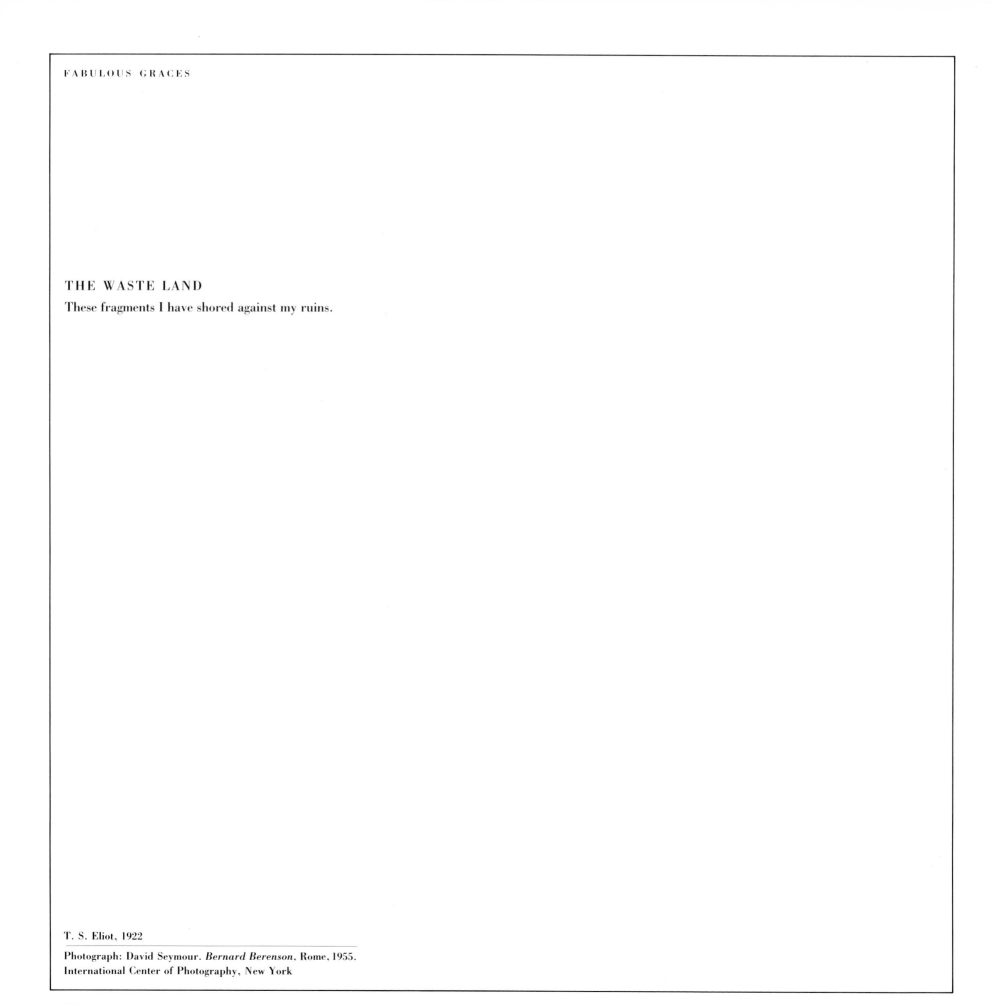

THE WASTE LAND

These fragments I have shored against my ruins.

T. S. Eliot, 1922

Photograph: David Seymour. *Bernard Berenson*, Rome, 1955.
International Center of Photography, New York

NOTES OF TRAVEL

Whatever beauty there may be in a Roman ruin is the remnant of what was beautiful originally; whereas an English ruin is more beautiful often in its decay than even it was in its primal strength. If we ever build such noble structures as these Roman ones, we can have just as good ruins, after two thousand years, in the United States.

Nathaniel Hawthorne, February 7, 1858

Photograph: Elliott Erwitt. *Rome*, 1959

LETTER TO WILLIAM H. PRESCOTT

As I am in the category of changes in Rome, I will give you another class of them,—I mean those that relate to ecclesiastical affairs and manners. The manners of the higher clergy, and probably of all classes of the clergy, are become more staid; perhaps their characters are improved, for I hear fewer stories to their discredit. The first time I was invited to the Borgheses', in 1836, was on a Sunday evening, and the first thing I saw when I entered was seven Cardinals, four at one table, three at another, with their red skull-caps and *pieds de perdrix*, playing at cards. Similar exhibitions I witnessed all the season through, there and elsewhere. But this year I have not seen a single Cardinal at a card-table. The Pope is known to disapprove it, and that is enough. . . . Indeed, though ecclesiastics of all the higher ranks go into fashionable society still, and even to balls, their numbers are smaller, and they go early and leave soon.

George Ticknor, January 25, 1857

Photograph: Mario Giacomelli. *No Hands Caress My Face*, Rome, 1961–63

FOR THE NEW RAILWAY STATION IN ROME

What city is eternal
But that which prints itself within the groping head
Out of the blue unbroken reveries
    Of the building dead?

What is your praise of pride
But to imagine excellence, and try to make it?
What does it say over the door to Heaven
    But *homo fecit*?

Richard Wilbur, 1956

Photograph: Elliott Erwitt. *Via Appia*, 1959

LETTER TO JOHN SINGLETON COPLEY

Dear Sir,

Some days past Your Brother Mr. Clark delivered into my hands your letter of 8th of Novr., Which informed me of your intended Tour into Italy, and the desier you express'd of receiveing my Opinion on that Subject. I am still of the opinion the going to Italy must be of the greatest advantage to one advanced in the arts as you are, As by that you will find what you are already in possession of, and what you have to acquier.

As your jurney to Italy is reather to finish a studye then to begin one, Your stay in that country will not requier that length of time that would be necessary for an Artist less advanced in the Arts then you are; But I would have that time as uninterrupted as possible. And for this reason I would have you make this Tour without Mrs. Copley. Not that she would be of any great aditional expance, But would reather bring you into a mode of liveing that would throw you out of your Studyes. So my Advice is, Mrs. Copley to remain in Boston till you have made this Tour, After which, if you fix your place of reasidanc in London, Mrs. Copley to come over.

In regard to your studyes in Italy my advice is as follows: That you pursue the higher Exalances in the Art, and for the obtaining of which I recommend to your attention the works of the *Antiant Statuarys, Raphael, Michal Angilo, Corragio*, and *Titian*, as the Sorce from whance true tast in the arts have flow'd. There ware a number of great artists in Italy besides thoss, But as they somewhat formd their manner in paint from the above artists, they are but second place painters. The works of the Antient Statuarys are the great original whare in the various charectors of nature are finely represented, from the soundest principles of Philosophi. What they have done in Statuary, Raphael seems to have acquiered in painting. In him you see the fine fancey in the arraignment of his figures into groops, and those groops into a whole with that propriety and fitness to his subject, Joynd to a trouth of charector and expression, that was never surpass'd before nor sence. Michal Angilo in the knowledge and graundor of the Human figure has surpass'd all artists. His figures have the apearance of a new creation, form'd by the strength of his great amagination. In him you find all that is great in design. Corragio, whose obscurety in life deprived him of those aids in the art which Michal Angilo and Raphael had, and which prevented his acquiering those Exalances, which so charectoris'd them. But there are other beuties in the art he greatly surpass'd even those in and all others that came after him. Which was in the relieaf of his figures by the management of the clear obscure. The prodigious management in foreshortning of figures seen in the air, The greacefull smiles and turnes of heads, The magickcal uniteing of his Tints, The incensable blending of lights into Shades, and the beautyfull affect over the whole arrising from thoss pices of management, is what charmes the eye of every beholder. Titian gave the Human figure that trouth of colour which surpass'd all other painters. His portraits have a particular air of grandour and a solidity of coloring in them that makes all other portraits appear trifling. I recommend to your attention when in Italy that workes of the above artists, as every perfection in the art of painting is to be found in one or another of their works.

Benjamin West, London, January 6, 1773

Photograph: Aaron Traub. *Italian Art*, Florence, 1981

ITALY BY LAND AND BY SEA

How could historical change and displacement have stripped Venice, once a place and symbol of such great significance, to such a degree? The history of Venice has come to a halt, and it may have occurred precisely in order to preserve with splendor the remnants of that great history. To be fixed and eternal, Venice had to be dead. The Egyptians may have come across the idea of the mummy in the same way; one can well imagine how, for those among them who were most logically inclined, life could only have attained its full value in the elaborate, uncorrupt silence of the embalmed sepulcher. Certainly a great repulsion and sense of sadness would have befallen those people had they foreseen that one day air would once again filter through and spoil the fragile mummies. It would have been like forcing them to believe in death, to recognize it as the ultimate victor. We, too, would have liked to select and preserve some precious image.

Riccardo Bacchelli, 1918

Photograph: Gregory Benson. *Venice*, 1981

NOTES OF TRAVEL

Death strides behind every man, to be sure, at more or less distance, and, sooner or later, enters upon any event of his life; so that, in this point of view, they might each and all serve for bas-reliefs on a sarcophagus; but the Romans seem to have treated Death as lightly and playfully as they could, and tried to cover his dart with flowers, because they hated it so much.

Nathaniel Hawthorne, May 12, 1858

Photograph: Mimmo Jodice. *Gorgoneion*, Naples, 1982

INVISIBLE CITIES

When a man rides a long time through wild regions he feels the desire for a city. Finally he comes to Isidora, a city where the buildings have spiral staircases encrusted with spiral seashells, where perfect telescopes and violins are made, where the foreigner, hesitating between two women, always encounters a third, where cockfights degenerate into bloody brawls among the bettors. He was thinking of all these things when he desired a city. Isidora, therefore, is the city of his dreams: with one difference. The dreamed-of city contained him as a young man; he arrives at Isidora in his old age. In the square there is the wall where the old men sit and watch the young go by; he is seated in a row with them. Desires are already memories.

Italo Calvino, 1974

Photograph: Gregory Benson. *On the Train to Florence*, 1981

ROBA DI ROMA

My friend Count Cignale is a painter; he has a wonderful eye for color and exquisite taste. He was making me a visit the other day, and in strolling about in the neighborhood we were charmed with an old stone wall of as many colors as Joseph's coat: tender grays, dashed with creamy yellows and golden greens, and rich subdued reds, were mingled together in its plastered stonework; above towered a row of glowing oleanders covered with clusters of roseate blossoms. Nothing would do but that he must paint it and so secure it at once for his portfolio; for who knows, said he, that the owner will not take it into his head to whitewash it next week and ruin it? So he painted it, and a beautiful picture it made. Within a week the owner made a call on us. He had seen Cignale painting his wall, with surprise, and deemed an apology necessary. "I am truly sorry," he said, "that the wall is left in such a condition. It ought to be painted all over with a uniform tint, and I will do it at once. I have long had this intention, and I will no longer omit to carry it into effect."

"Let us beseech you," we both cried at once, "*caro conte mio*, to do no such thing, for you will ruin your wall. What! whitewash it over! it is profanation, sacrilege, murder, and arson."

He opened his eyes. "Ah! I did not mean to whitewash it, but to wash it over with a pearl color," he said.

William Wetmore Story, 1887

Photograph: Mario Cresci. *House in Basilicata*, 1980

THE LEGACY OF ITALY

The Italian joy of living was also reflected in a refinement and enjoyment of the simple life. During the Renaissance, table manners and the use of the fork, the rules of fencing and horseback riding were principally discoveries of Italian origin. But pre-eminent was the enjoyment of wit, conversation, repartee, social gathering, human interests, and therefore the theater and other forms of social living in which Italians, born actors and famous conversationalists, excelled. The capacity to enjoy oneself and to amuse others with gestures is a typically Italian characteristic, which people with less mobile features look on with secret envy, even when they speak of it with seeming contempt.

Giuseppe Prezzolini, 1948

ITALIAN HOURS

The faculty of making much of common things and converting small occasions into great pleasures is, to a son of communities strenuous as ours are strenuous, the most salient characteristic of the so-called Latin civilizations. It charms him and vexes him, according to his mood; and for the most part it represents a moral gulf between his own temperamental and indeed spiritual sense of race, and that of Frenchmen and Italians, far wider than the watery leagues that a steamer may annihilate. But I think his mood is wisest when he accepts the "foreign" easy surrender to all the senses as the sign of an unconscious philosophy of life, instilled by the experience of centuries—the philosophy of people who have lived long and much, who have discovered no short cuts to happiness and no effective circumvention of effort.

Henry James, 1909

Photograph: Mitch Epstein. *Florence*, 1979

ITALY AND THE ITALIANS

I have seen and heard much of an Italian love of music, but nothing illustrates it so forcibly as an incident that occurred last evening at the opera. In the midst of one of the scenes, a man in the pit near the orchestra was suddenly seized with convulsions. His limbs stiffened; his eyes became set in his head, and stood wide open, staring at the ceiling like the eyes of a corpse, while low and agonizing groans broke from his struggling bosom. The prima-donna came forward at that moment, but seeing this livid, death-stamped face before her, suddenly stopped, with a tragic look and start that for *once* was perfectly natural. She turned to the bass-singer, and pointed out the frightful spectacle. He also started back in horror and the prospect was that the opera would terminate on the spot; but the scene that was just opening was the one in which the prima-donna was to make her great effort, and around which the whole effort was gathered, and the spectators were determined not to be disappointed because one man was dying, and so shouted, "Go on! Go on!" Clara Novello gave another look toward the groaning man, whose whole aspect was enough to freeze the blood, and then started off in her part. But the dying man grew worse and worse, and finally sprung bolt upright in his seat. A person sitting behind him, all absorbed in the music, immediately placed his hands on his shoulders, pressed him down again, and held him firmly in his place. There he sat, pinioned fast, with his pale, corpselike face upturned, in the midst of that gay assemblage, and the foam rolling over his lips, while the braying of trumpets, and the voice of the singer, drowned the groans that were rending his bosom. At length the foam became streaked with blood as it oozed through his teeth, and the convulsive starts grew quicker and fiercer. But the man behind held him fast, while he gazed in perfect rapture on the singer, who now, like the ascending lark, was trying her loftiest strain. As it ended the house rang with applause, and the man who had held down the poor dying creature could contain his ecstasy no longer, and lifting his hands from his shoulders, clapped them rapidly together three or four times, crying out over the ears of the dying man, "Brava, brava!" and then hurriedly placing them back again to prevent his springing up in his convulsive throes. It was a perfectly maddening spectacle, and the music jarred on the chords of my heart like the blows of a hammer. But the song was ended, the effect secured, and so the spectators could attend to the sufferer in their midst. The gens-d'armes entered, and carried him speechless and lifeless out of the theater.

Joel Tyler Headley, 1844

Photograph: Giorgio Lotti. *Teatro alla Scala*, Milan, 1973

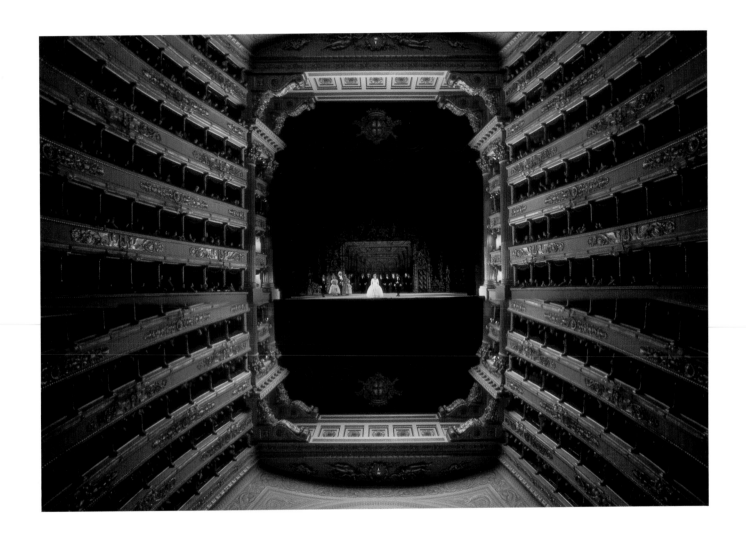

THE BELLA LINGUA

The beauty of Italy is not easy to come by any longer, if it ever was, but, driving to a villa below Anticoli for a weekend with friends, Streeter saw a country of such detail and loveliness that it could not be described. They had reached the villa early on a rainy night. Nightingales sang in the trees, the double doors of the villa stood open, and in all the rooms there were bowls of roses and olive-wood fires. It had seemed, with the servants bowing and bringing in candles and wine, like some gigantic and princely homecoming in a movie, and, going out onto the terrace after dinner to hear the nightingales and see the lights of the hill towns, Streeter felt that he had never been put by dark hills and distant lights into a mood of such tenderness. In the morning, when he stepped out onto his bedroom balcony, he saw a barefoot maid in the garden, picking a rose to put in her hair. Then she began to sing. It was like a flamenco—first guttural and then falsetto—and poor Streeter found his Italian still so limited that he couldn't understand the words of the song, and this brought him around to the fact that he couldn't quite understand the landscape, either. His feeling about it was very much what he might have felt about some excellent resort or summer place—a scene where, perhaps as children, we have thrown ourselves into a temporary relationship with beauty and simplicity that will be rudely broken off on Labor Day. It was the evocation of a borrowed, temporary, bittersweet happiness that he rebelled against—but the maid went on singing, and Streeter did not understand a word.

John Cheever, 1964

Photograph: Mario Giacomelli. *Story of the Land*, 1980

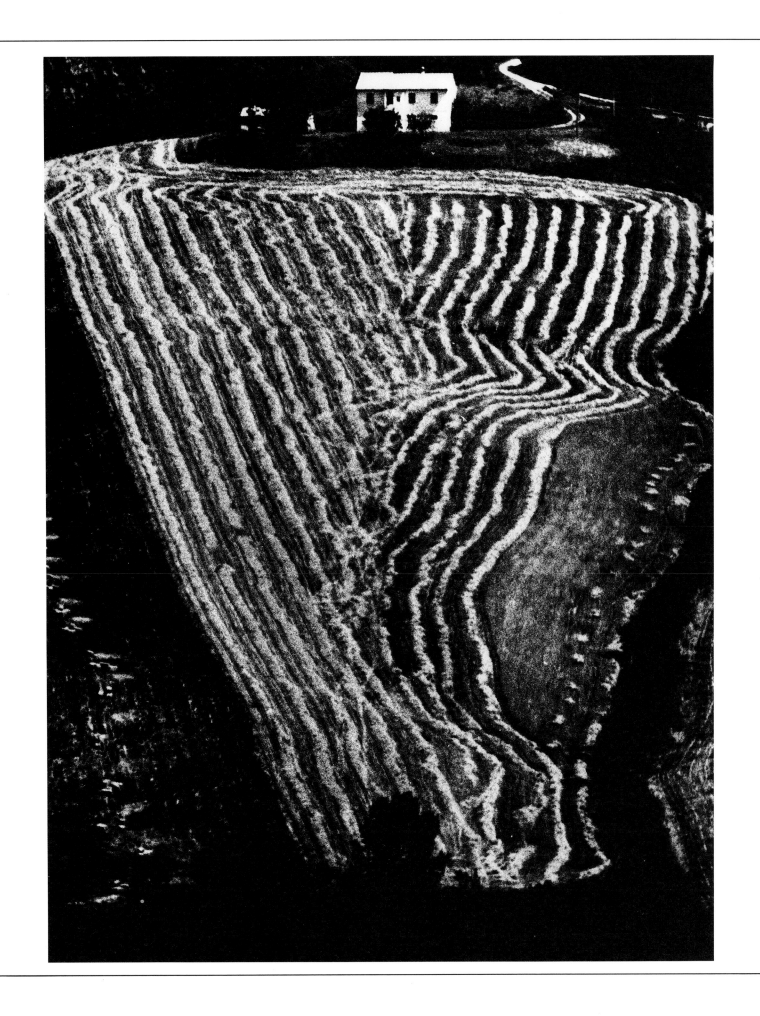

THE REAL ITALIANS

But what can foreigners know about the Italian soul and its relation to nature, when, supplied with documents from the libraries, they devote to the Lombard or Tuscan countryside only the tour indicated by the asterisks in Baedeker? I am Italian; I passed all my childhood and youth in the country. But I must admit that I understood the long silences and fixed gaze of the Italian peasants for the first time only when I remembered them in China, where also the love of the land assumes an almost religious tenderness. It is easy to become ecstatic about the crowds of Japanese who swarm, almost as if on pilgrimage, to the valleys of flowering cherry trees or, in summer, scramble with emotion up the shifting trails of Fujiyama. For that, like the exaltation of the Germans for what still remains unconquered in nature, cannot fail to stir the dullest imagination. But the Chinaman discovers in his fields a beauty of which he never tires: he sets before the tablets of his ancestors bread from wheat that has ripened in the same rows his father cultivated; and on the rare occasions when he feels called to pray, he prefers the rustic image of some god sheltered under a poor shaky arch near his own fields to the gilded statues of the neighboring city. This is what the Italian feels for the light oil of his olives and the white and red wines from his few square yards of vineyard. These are the rewards of his deep-rooted union with an earth which no longer holds any terror for him and with which he has contracted a sort of secret marriage. His silent, solemn love has none of the ecstasy of German romanticism: it does not isolate the individual; it is latent in the minds of all Italians. It is capable of inspiring familial and patriotic tenderness, not the anguish and nostalgia of uneasy souls dreaming of a return to the life of pure instinct. Whereas infinite forests and tumultuous rivers inspire the northerner's disgust for too tangible frontiers, the Italian countryside has been linked for hundreds of years with the cycles of the farming seasons, changing from moon to moon. Even the remains of our popular poetry falls in with them. The last remnant of our mystery plays, performed in the public squares of Tuscan villages in spring, is called the *Maggio* (Maytime). These feelings, already more collective than individual and as profound then as they are now, were in the mind of Horace when he wrote *Inveni portum.* Can it be that the discomfiture of the German mind comes from its inability to find the portum which the Italians have made the ideal of their lives?

Carlo Sforza, 1942

Photograph: Monica Fritz. *Radda, in Chianti,* 1982

LETTER TO THE ARTIST'S WIFE

Though I have had no new orders or sales, I feel somehow encouraged. I have painted two pretty large pictures, and feel a good deal of satisfaction in them, and in the praises of the artists and visitors who have seen them. My forest scene is about finished, the best forest picture I have ever done. You remember the study,—that shady one, with the large beeches on the right. I have opened the woods a little on the left with a little bit of blue sky and dim horizon—two figures in the distance. The beech trunks are painted firm and round and mossy and full of color and impasto, also the oaks and the foliage thoroughly leafy and loose, the chief light being strong sunshine between the trees. The ground is solid and the dry leaves well indicated. You can walk right into the picture. On the whole it pleases me better than anything I have done. Page saw it the other day and praised it much. Several artists have done the same,—I want it to go to New York. I will show them that I can paint trees as well as some others over there.

Christopher Pearse Cranch, Rome, December 15, 1859

WAY BACK THERE THE VOID

Way back there the void, a fictitious mist of dingy light.
The indistinct will swallow you up. Stop here amidst the dying
weeds of discolored sun. The swampy sky is cut out from shadows
shaped incongruously like huge trees, threatening
sentries of the gaping green.
You cannot say whether it is a garden abandoned to desolation
or an uncultivated corner of restless vegetation. Those black,
still giants are drawn in a fragile pattern—slender trunks and lithe
branches—already distraught by melancholy. Stop
and turn back. Here nothing can be said. There is nothing
to dig into. This is a haunting place, rotting
and thickening in solitude. The ghostly light
allows no one else this indiscretion.

Alfredo Giuliani, Rome, 1988

Photograph: Ray K. Metzker. *Leaf Festival*, Castagneto, Tuscany, 1985

Disfigured Myth EXHIBITS THE IRONIC, SELF-CRITICAL

style of that surprises Italy's admiring visitor. Even as the myth of Italy continues to shed its attractive light, the country simultaneously suffers the typical insecurities of a modern, unisolated culture. Comparison of its ways and mores with those of other Western nations results in a humorous acceptance of contradictions. As activity and resignation coexist, so, too, skepticism and passion ambiguously interplay.

FRATELLI D'ITALIA

For me, the starting point of the grand tour to Italy is still Germany, Franconia, while the arrival is Mediterranean. Here, too, however, one could not be further removed from Goethe. . . . We are dealing with a black and gold, Hoffmannlike Italy, haunted by masks and ghosts and hallucinations occurring in broad daylight.

Alberto Arbasino, 1967

Photograph: Geri della Rocca de Candal. *Venice in Winter*, 1977

MICHAEL ANGELO: A FRAGMENT

Michael Angelo:
So, Benvenuto, you return once more
To the Eternal City. T'is the center
To which all gravitates. One finds no rest
Elsewhere than here. There may be other cities
That please us for a while, but Rome alone
Completely satisfies. It becomes to all
A second native land by predilection,
And not by accident of birth alone.

Benvenuto:
I am but just arrived, and am now lodging
With Bindo Altoviti. I have been
To kiss the feet of our most Holy Father,
And now am come in haste to kiss the hands
Of my miraculous Master.

Henry Wadsworth Longfellow, 1872

Photograph: Luigi Ghirri. *Theme Park*, Rimini, 1977

FOTO
RICORDO
a colori
pronte in 1 minuto

ITALIAN JOURNEYS

Pleasant Count Baldassare Castiglione! whose incomparable book of the *Cortigiano* succeeded in teaching his countrymen every gentlemanly grace but virtue.

William Dean Howells, 1872

Photograph: Gabriele Basilico. Untitled, from *Dancing in Emilia*, 1980

PORTRAITS OF PLACES

The misery of Venice stands there for all the world to see; it is part of the spectacle—a thoroughgoing devotee of local color might consistently say it is part of the pleasure. The Venetian people have little to call their own—little more than the bare privilege of leading their lives in the most beautiful of towns.

Their habitations are decayed; their taxes heavy; their pockets light; their opportunities few. One receives an impression, however, that life presents itself to them with attractions not accounted for in this meager train of advantages, and that they are on better terms with it than many people who have made a better bargain. They lie in the sunshine; they dabble in the sea; they wear bright rags; they fall into attitudes and harmonies; they assist at an eternal *conversazione*. It is not easy to say that one would have them other than they are, and it certainly would make an immense difference should they be better fed. The number of persons in Venice who evidently never have enough to eat is painfully large; but it would be more painful if we did not equally perceive that the rich Venetian temperament may bloom upon a dog's allowance. Nature has been kind to it, and sunshine and leisure and conversation and beautiful views form the greater part of its sustenance. It takes a great deal to make a successful American; but to make a happy Venetian takes only a handful of quick sensibility. The Italian people have, at once, the good and evil fortune to be conscious of few wants; so that if the civilization of a society is measured by the number of its needs, as seems to be the common opinion of today, it is to be feared that the children of the lagoon would make but a poor figure in a set of comparative tables. Not their misery, doubtless, but the way they elude their misery, is what pleases the sentimental tourist, who is gratified by the sight of a beautiful race that lives by the aid of its imagination. The way to enjoy Venice is to follow the example of these people and make the most of simple peasures. Almost all the pleasures of the place are simple; this may be maintained even under the imputation of ingenious paradox. There is no simpler pleasure than looking at a fine Titian—unless it be [a] look at a fine Tintoret, or strolling into St. Mark's—it is abominable, the way one falls into the habit—and resting one's light-wearied eyes upon the windowless gloom; or than floating in a gondola, or hanging over a balcony, or taking one's coffee at Florian's. It is of these superficial pastimes that a Venetian day is composed, and the pleasure of the matter is in the emotions to which they minister.

Henry James, 1883

Photograph: Charles Traub. *Venice*, 1980

THE ITALIANS

There are not too many of them. They have something growing on them, some of them, a good many of them, and certainly very many others would not be wanting such things to be growing out of them that is to say growing on them. It makes them, those having such things, makes them elegant and charming, makes them ugly and disgusting, makes them clean looking and sleek and rich and dark, makes them dirty looking and fierce and annoying.

Gertrude Stein, 1922

Photograph: William Klein. *Barbershop*, Rome, 1956

THE LEGACY OF ITALY

The word *ventura* in Italian means fate or fortune; the adventurer is one who believes in the God of the skeptics—luck. It is a name that several Italians have applied to themselves or to other eminent men: Goldoni called himself the Honored Adventurer, D'Annunzio, the Adventurer without Adventure, and Garibaldi, especially in the early part of his life, was referred to as an Adventurer. Even before the word became popular, the description fitted certain humanists like Buonarroti (Callimaco Esperiente) and in various moments of their lives, some discoverers and travelers like Columbus and Marco Polo.

*The Callimaco Esperiente the author refers to may be Filippo Buonaccorsi (1437–1496), who as Polish ambassador to Constantinople, Venice, and Rome demonstrated his humanist tendencies through his historical writings, letters, orations, and poetry.

Giuseppe Prezzolini, 1948

Photograph: Roy Gumpel. *Sailor*, Venice, 1983

MY HOST THE WORLD

When at the threshold of old age I found myself free and looked about for a place of retirement and finally found it in Italy and particularly in Rome, I was not at all in search of an ideal society or even of a congenial one. I was looking only for suitable lodgings, where the climate, the scene, and the human ways of my neighbors might not impede but if possible inspire me in my projected work and where I might bring my life to a peaceful end. As to society, I was quite content with that which naturally surrounded me; for I still had my family and my friends in America, in England, and in Spain; while in Italy later, the Anglo-American residents, with their fringe of distinguished Italian acquaintances, would have been accessible to me if I had cared to cultivate them more assiduously. But essentially I desired solitude and independence: not in the English form of quiet home life in the country, but rather after the fashion of ancient philosophers, often in exile, but always in sight of the marketplace and the theater.

George Santayana, ca. 1950

Photograph: A. Doren. *Espresso*, Florence, 1979

PISAN CANTOS

I believe in the resurrection of Italy   *quia impossibile est.*

Ezra Pound, 1948

Photograph: William Klein. *Excavation of Cinecittà*, Rome, 1956

THE INNOCENTS ABROAD

At two in the morning we swept through the Straits of Messina, and so bright was the moonlight that Italy on the one hand and Sicily on the other seemed almost as distinctly visible as though we looked at them from the middle of a street we were traversing. The city of Messina, milk-white, and starred and spangled all over with gaslights, was a fairy spectacle. A great party of us were on deck smoking and making a noise, and waiting to see famous Scylla and Charybdis. And presently the Oracle stepped out with his eternal spyglass and squared himself on the deck like another Colossus of Rhodes. It was a surprise to see him abroad at such an hour. Nobody supposed he cared anything about an old fable like that of Scylla and Charybdis. One of the boys said:

"Hello, doctor, what are you doing up here at this time of night?—What do you want to see this place for?"

"What do I want to see this place for? Young man, little do you know me, or you wouldn't ask such a question. I wish to see all the places that's mentioned in the Bible."

"Stuff! This place isn't mentioned in the Bible."

"It ain't mentioned in the Bible!—this place ain't—well, now, what place is this, since you know so much about it?"

"Why it's Scylla and Charybdis."

"Scylla and Cha—confound it, I thought it was Sodom and Gomorrah!"

Mark Twain, 1869

Photograph: Roberto Salbitani. Untitled, Florence, from *The Invasion of the City*, 1973

CUORE: AN ITALIAN SCHOOLBOY'S JOURNAL

Why "never more," Enrico? That will depend on yourself. When you have finished the fourth grade, you will go to the Gymnasium, and [your school-mates] will become workingmen; but you will remain in the same city for many years, perhaps. Why then, will you never meet again? When you are in the University or the Lyceum, you will seek them out in their shops or their work-rooms, and it will be a great pleasure for you to meet the companions of your youth once more, as men at work. I should like to see you neglecting to look up Coretti or Precossi, wherever they may be! And you will go to them, and you will pass hours in their company, and you will see, when you come to study life and the world, how many things you can learn from them, which no one else is capable of teaching you, both about their arts and their society and your own country. And have a care; for if you do not preserve these friendships, it will be extremely difficult for you to acquire other similar ones in the fu-ture,—friendships, I mean to say, outside of the class to which you belong; and thus you will live in one class only; and the man who associates with but one social class is like the student who reads but one book.

Edmondo de Amicis, 1887

Photograph: Leo Rubinfien. *The Train to Milan*, 1982

OUR LADY OF THE TURKS

There are idiots who have seen the Virgin Mary, and there are idiots who have not seen the Virgin Mary. "I am an idiot who has never seen the Virgin Mary." At this point he perched on top of two cushions, and leaning forward, not without visible effort, he continued: "It comes to this, either one sees the Virgin Mary or one doesn't see her." Suddenly, he glanced around at his red-capped audience and finding them still attending to the previous remarks, he threatened to have them taken away. Then a wing of youth spread out among the elders, fanned by a threat as palpable as a migraine, moving as if the council had recessed for coffee. There was no more coffee in the house. All poured themselves something to drink, most of them taking sweet liqueurs. They drank in celebration, sitting in a circle around his awesome presence, as if paying a visit to some bedridden, illustrious personage. They were in a state of suspension, and between their two fingers delicately held two drops of rosolio as if they were live butterflies. To see or not to see the Virgin Mary—the sick man pronounced again—that is the theme. He amused them for a long while with the story of Brother Ass, St. Joseph of Cupertino, who tended the pigs; he fashioned wings for himself out of his own awkwardness, and at night, in prayer, he flew around the altar of the Virgin with his mouth agape. The idiots who see the Virgin Mary suddenly have wings; they also know how to fly and alight like a feather. The idiots who don't see the Virgin have no wings, are unfit to fly, and yet they fly just the same. Instead of landing, they fall like one having lead at his ankles and wanting to free himself of it, decides to cut off his feet. Then he drags himself toward salvation, amid the mockery of the guardians, who rightfully trust that the imminent hemorrhage will stop him. But those who see don't see what they see, those who fly are themselves the flight. We don't know who it is that flies. Such a miracle annihilates them: rather than seeing the Virgin Mary, they are the Virgin they see. This paradoxical, insane identity that empties the praying one of his subject and in exchange deludes him into objectifying himself within another object, all this is ectasy. God is all that is different. If you want to embrace, you are the embrace; when you kiss, you are the mouth.

Carmelo Bene, 1978

Photograph: Mitch Epstein. *Hotel Berchielli*, Florence, 1977

ROME

The Abbott Fea, who was Provost for the Conservation of Monuments in Rome a couple of centuries ago, one day ordered certain huts flanking the right wing of the Pantheon to be torn down. (Supervisors of the Beaux Arts, let this not give you courage; huts are the best friends of monuments.) But in Abbott Fea's case, it seemed, there was a good reason to do so, for otherwise they would have fallen down on their own. After this, for a long stretch of time the grounds at the foot of the hyperbolical colonnade and along the side of the gigantic, round edifice remained in a state of restoration, but (as still happens today) were never restored. This plot lent itself wonderfully to the "convenience" of the people of the neighborhood—perhaps because of their love for the open air or because they lacked certain comforts in their houses—as well as to all the people passing by those parts who felt an urgent need. For many, many years the road, which when finally broadened and restored was called and is still called today the street of the Rotonda, was referred to by the Romans, upper and lower classes alike, as "Fea's shit hole," even when the Abbott Fea was no longer among us. Never mind the fact that "shit hole" might refer to the person carrying out a certain act and "shithouse" is the place where the act is carried out. We are not here to raise arid and pedantic questions about purity in the philological field, Lord protect us; so long as words are pronounced they have good reasons to exist, and they are wrong only when no longer pronounced.

Aldo Palazzeschi, 1920

Photograph: Mitch Epstein. *Arch of Constantine*, Rome, 1982

JOURNAL ENTRY

I am speedily satisfied with Venice. It is a great oddity, a city for beavers, but, to my thought, a most disagreeable residence. You feel always in prison, and solitary. Two persons may live months in adjoining streets and never meet, for you go about in gondolas, and all the gondolas are precisely alike, and the persons within commonly concealed; then there are no newsrooms; except St. Mark's Piazza, no place of public resort. It is as if you were always at sea.

Ralph Waldo Emerson, June 2, 1833

Photograph: Len Jenshel. *Venice*, 1985

THE ATHEIST AT THE GATE

The sad controversy over the doors of the Duomo at Orvieto could only have ended as it did—in a dialogue among the deaf—because each of the parties involved was using a different code. Let us assume, first of all, the point of view of the critics and art historians who served as members of the High Council of the Ministry of Education; having expressed a negative opinion and then been contradicted by the Minister, they resigned in protest. They are capable, authoritative people, all above suspicion. They have acted according to conscience. But it will be interesting to see what type of conscience we are dealing with.

It was a secular conscience, one that has replaced the cult of a missing God with the cult of art. A church, no longer being the house of someone who is missing, is, above all, a work of art. As such it is an absolute and must be run according to aesthetic rules. I read the superb article "Janua Coeli" by Cesare Brandi in the *Corriere della Sera*, in which he analyzes the stylistic reasons why Manzu's doors are well situated in St. Peter's while those by Greco are not fit for the Duomo at Orvieto. Brandi deduces his reasons according to a logic of style. And by this logic, he is right. But this logic of artistic style is "contemporary": it implies that the work of art has an autonomous and untouchable value, that it has its own code, and that it cannot tolerate any deviation. But an abstract work of art is a modern invention, a religious solution elaborated by an atheistic society. The fact that we all follow this religion does not matter here. One must also bring to trial the myths in which one believes. In past eras a church could be changed with great ease. Eventually posterity would take it upon itself to define its homogeneity or to point out the exquisite contradiction between Gothic naves, let us say, and Romanesque facades. And now let us go on to consider the problem from the point of view of the believer. For him, a church is not simply a work of art: it is the house of the children of God, and as such it lives for the life of its children, who bend its architectural structure to suit their needs. It is not a museum but something like a railway station or hospital. As a living house for the children of God, the Duomo at Orvieto should have the doors that suit it best. For instance, since there is a continuous coming and going of people into the church, permitting cold air to enter and making the faithful cold, why not furnish it with revolving doors? The critics need not worry; within a hundred years we will find the doors beautiful. But better yet, a Duomo should have no outside doors at all; the faithful should see what is going on inside and be enticed to participate in the rites with those who have entered; in order to avoid the cold it would suffice to install, as in certain northern restaurants, a screen of hot air on the threshold capable of inducing in the faithful warm feelings at once inviting and endearing. So what if thieves should enter at night? A church should be open all day and all night in order to receive the solitary and hopeless as well as groups of believers; and it should give hospitality to those who have no roofs over their heads, without forcing them to sleep hidden away in the waiting rooms of the station. But since this life of the faithful does not exist around the Duomo, and since the Duomo is, rather, an artistic object for the tourists, the Church must enter into the atheistic logic of art criticism and decide to make the monument more "aesthetic."

But why make it more aesthetic by introducing, little by little, works of modern sacred art into an object of ancient sacred art? Simply to demonstrate the vitality of the institution through an operation of public relations, like Olivetti or Pirelli when they commission a calendar by a well-known graphic artist. But when Olivetti, instead, has a new typewriter designed, aesthetic needs are adapted to the functional ones. Yet the Church of Orvieto puts in a door that only "recalls" the function of the doors of times past: which contained reliefs for the simple reason that they, along with the other sculptures of the building, fulfilled the function of presenting information for a mass of believers lacking means of instruction. Today, other channels exist, and the temple could serve an instructive function by installing some television screens in the place of doors; the lives of the saints could be told on them; elements of sexual education could be broadcast, or the activities of the Indian sisters in the West could be documented. Instead to entrust the doors to a modern sculptor who is looking to reinterpret the sentiments of the medieval artisan means that we accept the secular and atheistic logic of aesthetic worth as an absolute value. And so it is necessary to agree with the High Council, which advises against the doors for purely stylistic reasons. It does not make sense to respond by stating that the Greco doors are a work of art. If that is the case, then this is precisely the reason why they do not fit.

Umberto Eco, 1973

Photographs: Olivo Barbieri.
Untitled and *Grado*, ca. 1980

LETTER TO AMERICA

We have had a great day here today, for we have got up the column in honor of the Immaculate Conception on its pedestal in front of the Propaganda. Since Fontana put up the obelisk in the Square of St. Peter's there has been no such undertaking here; the column is of *cipollino*, a beautiful piece of marble, once a part of some ancient ruin, but for hundreds of years it has been lying on the Quirinal. It is said that the Pope, tired of seeing it lie there, established the dogma of the Immaculate Conception in order to make use of the column. There was little ceremony today, but the raising was a great and ingenious work, and perfectly successful. The Pope was not present, and I hear that his presence was feared on account of his evil eye. He is a known *gettatore*. Queen Christina looked on from the Spanish Palace, and did no harm. There is no likelihood of trouble here this winter; the people, to be sure, are very poor, but also very broken up. They hate this column on which money is wasted while they starve; how much more [they hate] the Cardinals and the priests.

Charles Eliot Norton, December 8, 1856

Photograph: Aaron Siskind. *Rome*, 1963

LETTER TO THE PAINTER'S MOTHER

You can have no Idea how easy it is to travil in this Country, and none of those dangers or dificultys attend it which are immagined by People that have not been in Europe. It is only passing from one Town to another, as from Boston to Roxbury, and the whole way houses, and People ready to do what ever you may want. Roberys are very rarely known to be perpitrated, and so much security from things of this kind that people travil much more by night than Day in the warm weither. It is not so in England. The great dificultys that attend traviling here is that the people will impose on one if it is possible for them to do it; for there is no regulations for the Inns, and they will make the most of their Guests.

John Singleton Copley, June 25, 1775

Photograph: Gianni Berengo Gardin. *Venice*, 1960

Shattered Illusions TESTIFIES TO THE DULLED LUSTER OF

the Italian myth and the erosion of its power. The contradictions are unveiled, yet the assumptions of grandeur linger on. Sensing the irreconcilable rift between the responsibilities of the mythic legacy and the imminence of pragmatic concerns, the admirer becomes a witness.

THERE IS NO DEATH

The old gods brought us comfort,
Even if they were hostile.
The new ones may treat us with vile
Benevolence, but they ignore our lot.

Eugenio Montale, 1971–72

Photograph: Paul Solomon. *St. Peter's*, Rome, 1980

INTELLECTUALS AND THE PROGRAMMING OF CULTURE

Grammatical study of the Greek and Latin languages in the old school, where they were united respectively with the study of literature and political history, was an educative principle, in that the humanistic ideal embodied in Athens and Rome was diffused throughout society. It was an essential element of life and of national culture. Even the mechanics of the study of grammar was introduced from a cultural perspective. Individual ideas were not learned to attain an immediate practical or professional goal; the method appeared disinterested because the interest was in the inner development of the personality, the formation of character by means of the absorption and assimilation of the entire cultural past of modern European civilization. One did not learn Greek and Latin in order to speak the language—so as to become a waiter, interpreter, or business correspondent. One learned the languages in order to know the civilizations of the two peoples directly, considered necessary for modern civilization, so as to be oneself and to understand oneself consciously. The Latin and Greek languages were learned according to grammar, mechanically; but the charge of mechanicalness and aridity is to a large extent unjust and inaccurate. It is necessary to have young people acquire certain habits of diligence, of exactness, even of physical composure, of psychic concentration on predetermined subjects—all habits which cannot be acquired without the mechanical repetition of disciplines and methodical actions. Would a forty-year-old scholar be capable of sitting at a table for sixteen hours in succession if he had not, as a child, compulsorily, through mechanical coercion, assumed the appropriate psychophysical habits? If one wanted to produce some great scholars, it would be necessary to be concerned with the entire scholastic arena in order to succeed in bringing out those thousands or hundreds or even only dozens of scholars of great stamina that every civilization needs (if one can much improve in this field, with the aid of suitable scientific assistance, without returning to the scholastic methods of the Jesuits).

Antonio Gramsci, ca. 1930

Photograph: Gabriele Basilico. Untitled, from *Dancing in Emilia*, 1980

THE ASHES OF GRAMSCI

I'm not speaking of the individual, that
phenomenon of sensual and sentimental passions . . .
he has other vices; nor will I speak

of the name of his or its fatal destiny . . .
But oh the common prenatal vices
and the indisputable sins enmeshed

deep inside him! The actions, internal,
external, that incarnate him in life
are not immune to those

religions that, in life, mortgage
death, established to deceive
the light and shed light on the deceit.

Pier Paolo Pasolini, 1954

Photograph: Jerry Gordon. *Prayer*, Rome, 1983

THE ÆOLIANS

Inhabiting island, promontories, precious
strategic points
they learned the art
of trade and sea.
To obscure regions of the west
they carried the first
fabulous sparks of the spirit
stamped on ceramics
of nearby Anatolias.
They filled orders, exported
instruments for killing,
greenstones and basalt
for hatchets,
obsidian of a luminous black.
They loved strong winds,
seeing that time flies,
coin, barter,
fortune's goods.
While their strength held out
they were pirates.
Could they still have
a place in the City?
Hoers of exhausted land,
catchers of rotten fish.

Bartolo Cattafi, 1971

Photograph: Leonard Freed. *Sicily*, 1956

IN THE LAND OF THE POOR

They live in a state of light-hearted decadence. Once upon a time, many centuries ago, one of them called them all together, promising eternal riches in eternal freedom; that man was murdered and the kingdom he had spoken of was turned into a legend. To the poor those were the most beautiful days in their history, and out of a curious feeling of gratitude they strongly believe to this day that that man was beautiful. The legend, however, does not mention this at all.

Ennio Flaiano, 1956

Photograph: Thomas Roma. *Palermo*, 1982

ITALIAN ANTHROPOMETRY

Before the war, perhaps because of Walt Disney movies, the "cute" style began to contaminate almost every aspect of life—minor architecture, interior design, some women's fashions, the delicate, entreating painting of certain renowned women painters, the intentionally stammering, ingenuous prose of certain writers. It should be noted that the phenomenon was common to all European countries and to those living in the shadow of European civilization, from the totalitarian and socialistic countries to the liberal ones, from the military dictatorships to the parliamentary republics. Many country cottages began to resemble Hansel and Gretel's: certain interiors were adorned in a style that was called "rustic": tablecloths with red and white checks, furniture made of simple wood with spread legs, straw-filled chairs, cellophane lampshades decorated with little hand-painted flowers, cretonnes in vivid colors, red majolica ware, and more. (Mind you, this rustic style has nothing to do with the solid furniture used by farmers, who sleep in huge beds made of iron and brass and own chests of drawers, closets, and bread bins made of solid walnut, and inexpensive, rough, straw-bottomed chairs. It was a case of the artificial "rustic," comparable to the Arcadia of the poets or the dairies of Marie Antoinette.)

Luigi Barzini, 1973

Photograph: Mitch Epstein. *Boboli Gardens*, Florence, 1982

GILDA FROM VIA MACMAHON

The season for Cowboys and Indians was too short. Not enough time to savor the madness of those adventures, the confusion and noise and all that galloping, the atrocity of those deadly duels. Showdowns, gory fistfights, pow, bang, smack. And he was the winner, he was always winning. Even when he was about to lose: so close to losing in fact that one would think he had really lost. But not at all; it only seemed that way. Indeed there was only one winner, always the same, always he, as strong as ten bulls put together.

Giovanni Testori, 1975

Photograph: Roberto Salbitani. Untitled, from *The Invasion of the City*, 1973

WOMEN OF THE SHADOWS

"As for the women. Put any label you want on it. It amounts to the same thing: we do whatever no one else has done. That's what we're taught, that's what we're supposed to do. Men work and talk about politics. We do the rest. If we have to decide, that's fair too. Why should we do all the work and not decide? We decide, but we don't have to talk about it in the Piazza. Call that power, if you want to. To us it's just killing work. That's what our lives are. We're born knowing it. And these young girls—my girls, all the girls—they're spoiled. No, they're ruined. 'I want this,' 'I want that,' 'I have a right to this,' is all they know. They won't work. It's beneath them. The schools taught them that. Taught them their rights. Only there's no easy way to get them, so they're going to wait for the miracle. They may starve, waiting like *signore*. They don't know yet that this isn't a world of miracles. It's a world of work. It's that simple. If you want something, you work and sometimes even then. . . . They don't know yet that miracles only happen in church." And so the last word belongs to Chichella, which is as it should be.

Ann Cornelisen, 1976

Photograph: Burton S. Glinn. *Bari Street Scene*, 1963

WOMEN

Except for my mother's maternity, nothing about their obscure sex really seemed to matter much, and I certainly didn't bother to poke into any of their mysteries. The great deeds I loved to read about were always done by men, never by women. Adventure, war, and glory were all of them manly privileges. Women stood for love, and books talked about splendid, queenly women, but I had a suspicion that women like that, and even that marvelous feeling of love, were just something invented by books, nothing really true. The perfect hero really did exist, I saw the proof of it in my father. But as for wonderful women, queens of love, like those in books—I never saw a single one. Maybe love, passion—this burning business they kept talking about—was something quite impossible, fantastic.

Although I knew nothing about real women, the glimpses I got of them were quite enough to make me conclude that they had absolutely nothing in common with the women in books. Real women, I thought, weren't splendid or magnificent. They were little creatures who could never grow as big as men, and they spent their whole life shut up indoors; that's why they were so pale. All bundled up in the aprons, skirts, and petticoats that had to hide those mysterious bodies of theirs, they seemed to me misshapen, almost deformed. Always busy, bustling, and ashamed of themselves, maybe because they were so ugly, they padded around like downcast animals, without any of the elegance, the casualness, the freedom of men. They'd get together in groups and chatter, waving excitedly, glancing round for fear someone might overhear their secrets. What dull kinds of secrets they must have been! Childish things, of course! No Absolute Certainties could possibly interest them.

Their eyes were all the same color—black; their hair was always dark, rough, wild-looking. As far as I was concerned, they could keep as far from the House of the Guaglioni as they liked. I'd certainly never fall in love with one of them, or want to marry one.

Sometimes, though not very often, some foreign woman would come to the island, and go down to the beach and get undressed to bathe, without the slightest modesty, just like a man. Like everyone else on Procida, I wasn't the least bit curious about these foreign bathers. My father seemed to consider them ridiculous and hateful, and avoided the places where they bathed, just as I did; we'd have liked to chase them away, because we felt possessive about our beaches. And as for the women, no one even looked at them. As far as Procidans were concerned, as far as I was concerned, they weren't women at all, but crazy beasts come down from the moon. It never entered my head that their shameless bodies might be beautiful.

Well, that seems to cover almost all my views on women!

I thought of the fate of women. When a girl was born in Procida, the family was upset. As children they were no uglier than boys, not very different, but they had no hope of growing up into handsome heroes; their only hope was to marry a hero, to serve him, to carry on his name, to be his exclusive property, respected by everyone; and to have by him a fine son, just like his father.

My mother hadn't even had this satifaction. She'd only just had time to see her dark, and dark-eyed, son, as unlike her husband Wilhelm as possible; and if by any chance this son was destined (though dark) to become a hero, she wouldn't know it because she was dead.

Elsa Morante, 1952

Photograph: Mario Giacomelli. *Scanno*, the Abruzzi, 1957–59

ETYMOLOGIES

In the region of the Italian linguistic atlas that encompasses Sicily, the entry *puttana* (prostitute) subdivides into two main families: *buttana* and *bagasa*. To these, one must add two singularly provocative denominations: *Rebecca* and, most strikingly, *la serva di Dio* (God's servant).

Eliot Ness, Jr., 1988

Photograph: Charles Traub. *God's Servant*, Palermo, 1981

THE QUESTION OF PORTRAITS

This is the way it went: through various people the mayor and the deputy mayor had already dealt with the arrival the evening before. Up until that time, what with the Germans marching in and the Germans strolling around—when even the chief of police had said to Carminella, the woman who ran the restaurant: "Let me stay here," and started to get undressed, "because there are Germans in the piazza"—the mayor and his deputy had had their own problems to deal with.

There had been people going around taking names: of Master Innocenzo, of anyone who had been in America, and of Master Innocenzo's more hotheaded students.

"Are they coming?" asked the deputy. "They're coming," they told him. "The Germans are back."

The deputy ran to tell the town clerk to open up the city offices: "It's to be hidden there: wrap it up in paper and put it in a basket." He put Mussolini's portrait back in place, right next to the King's. After all, the wall looked better with the stucco crucifix in the middle.

The night before, the Florentine who ran the shop at the train station had come and said: "You see? The English are coming tomorrow!" The deputy had called the messenger. "And we have to leave that there?" the town clerk asked pointing at the King. "Doesn't the wall look ugly?"

The deputy: "To cover up the white space, don't we have a Madonna, a Christopher Columbus?"

The town clerk: "In the files, we have another King, just about the same size."

They made a few tries, Victor Emanuel II was fine, and so they put him up.

Rocco Scotellaro, 1956

Photograph: Olivo Barbieri. Untitled, Naples, 1982

NOTES FOR CANTO CXVII ET SEQ.

M'amour, m'amour
        what do I love and
        where are you?
That I lost my center
        fighting the world
The dreams clash
        and are shattered—
and that I tried to make a paradiso
                                terrestre.

Ezra Pound, 1969

Photograph: Vincenzo Castella. *Private Geography*, Naples, 1975

ISCHIA

I forget why we came here: Ischia. It was being very much talked about, though few people seemed actually to have seen it—except, perhaps, as a jagged blue shadow glimpsed across the water from the heights of its celebrated neighbor, Capri. Some people advised against Ischia and, as I remember, they gave rather spooky reasons: You realize that there is an active volcano? And do you know about the plane? A plane, flying a regular flight between Cairo and Rome, crashed on top an Ischian mountain; there were three survivors, but no one ever saw them alive, for they were stoned to death by goatherds intent on looting the wreckage.

Truman Capote, 1949

Photograph: Mimmo Jodice. *Panorama, with Capri*, 1987

LETTER TO THE NEW YORK TRIBUNE

I earnestly hope for some expression of sympathy from my country toward Italy. Take a good chance and do something; you have shown much good feeling toward the Old World in its physical difficulties,—you ought to do still more in its spiritual endeavor. This cause is OURS, above all others; we ought to show that we feel it to be so. At present there is no likelihood of war, but in case of it I trust the United States would not fail in some noble token of sympathy toward this country. The soul of our nation need not wait for its government; these things are better done by individuals. I believe some in the United States will pay attention to these words of mine, will feel that I am not a person to be kindled by a childish, sentimental enthusiasm, but that I must be sure I have seen something of Italy before speaking as I do. I have been here only seven months, but my means of observation have been uncommon. I have been ardently desirous to judge fairly, and had no prejudices to prevent; beside, I was not ignorant of the history and literature of Italy, and had some common ground on which to stand with its inhabitants, and hear what they have to say. In many ways Italy is of kin to us; she is the country of Columbus, of Amerigo, of Cabot. It would please me much to see a cannon here bought by the contributions of Americans, at whose head should stand the name of Cabot, to be used by the Guard for salutes on festive occasions, if they should be so happy as to have no more serious need. In Tuscany they are casting one to be called the "Gioberti," from a writer who has given a great impulse to the present movement. I should like the gift of America to be called AMERIGO, the COLUMBO, or the WASHINGTON. Please think of this, some of my friends, who still care for the eagle, the Fourth of July, and the old cries of hope and honor. See if there are any objections that I do not think of, and do something if it is well and brotherly. Ah! America, with all thy rich boons, thou hast a heavy account to render for the talent given; see in every way that thou be not found wanting.

Margaret Fuller Ossoli, Rome, October 18, 1847

Photograph: Adam Bartos. *Near Rimini*, 1981

ACROSS THE RIVER AND INTO THE TREES

"My colleague, who works at his hotel, says that he drinks three or four high-balls, and then writes vastly and fluently far into the night."

"I dare say that makes marvelous reading."

"I dare say," Ettore said. "But it was hardly the method of Dante."

"Dante was another *vieux con*," the Colonel said. "I mean as a man. Not as a writer."

"I agree," Ettore said. "I think you will find no one, outside of Firenze, who has studied his life who would not agree."

"Eff Florence," the Colonel said.

"A difficult maneuver," Ettore said. "Many have attempted it but very few have succeeded. Why do you dislike it, my Colonel?"

"Too complicated to explain. But it was the depot," he said deposito, "of my old regiment when I was a boy."

"That I can understand. I have my own reasons for disliking it, too. You know a good town?"

"Yes," said the Colonel. "This one. A part of Milano; and Bologna. And Bergamo."

Ernest Hemingway, 1950

Photograph: Gianni Berengo Gardin. *Milan*, ca. 1960

DIARY OF A DREAMER

I mingle with strollers on the Janiculum, and I get worried. I must talk to the mayor, I say to myself. All these tourists incessantly looking at Rome will inevitably wear out its panorama. We must protect it from the corrosive stares of tourists. Hundreds of thousands of them every year. It slowly wastes away, day after day, and in the end nothing will be left of it! I look over the wall, and I must admit that the panorama is already a bit smudged and worn out. Even those dime-operated binoculars must be abolished; the mayor must do something about it.

Luigi Malerba, Rome, May 7–8, 1976

Photograph: Mimmo Jodice. *Gibellina*, Sicily, 1982

TO THE ULTERIOR GODS

Today, in this city, there flow country folks, tribes, players, circuses, multi-colored animals, athletes, storytellers, jesters, priests of three religions, young newlyweds, old libertines, children on their first visit to the den of vice, exotic merchants, drunkards, drug addicts, musicians, and healers. The crowds are so thick that the streets of the city are a glutinous dough of things human, a ubiquitous smell of sweat and urine, noise. I could destroy the city with an earthquake, a plague, a fire, a flood. I'll apply these means of death one by one: a third of the houses will crumble from the shock of the infuriated earth, a third will be consigned to flames, a third to the waters; part of those who escape will be killed by plunderers, part consumed by the plague; finally, a band of angels will efface the very name of the city from history, will make the ground of its foundations as smooth as a stone levigated by water. From my own fiction I will save a jester who can tell me with colorful inexactitude about the end of the great city, on that day of glory and splendor. Then I will even efface my friend the jester.

Giorgio Manganelli, 1972

Photograph: Bruce Cratsley. *Rising Water*, Venice, 1980

Extant Realism EXAMINES THE ORIGINS OF SUFFER-
ing in the hope that sacrifice and attempts at redemption may be all the better
understood. Realism is but one face of the coin of illusion. Myth provides the
necessary currency for a culture to negotiate the image of its own legacy. The
witness's immediate focus on jarringly factual concerns draws attention away
from the ethos arising even out of the banal.

YOU SHOULD NEVER ASK

Essentially, old age will mean the end of wonder. We will lose the ability to wonder ourselves and also to make others wonder. Having passed our whole lives marveling at everything, we will have nothing more to marvel at; and other people will no longer marvel at us, either because they've seen us do and say strange things before or because they won't be looking our way.

We could turn out to be scraps of junk abandoned in the grass or glorious ruins devotedly visited; actually, changeable and capricious as fate is, we might sometimes be one and sometimes the other; but in either case we will have no more wonder; our imagination, old as a lifetime, will have already made use of and consumed in its bosom every possible event and every change of fortune: and whether junk or illustrious ruins, we will elicit no wonder in either case: there is no significant wonder in the devotion lavished on antiquity and even less in stumbling upon some scrap of junk rusting in the midst of nettles. Besides, there is no significant difference between either: for in both cases the warm river of days flows upon other banks.

Natalia Ginzburg, 1976

Photograph: Gianni Berengo Gardin. *Rome*, 1977

FOR GIANFRANCO

I have no wish to die today, I don't even
have the hope of dying today: I am in the throes of full
cerebral activity; I am like the others—

candid, for your death strewn with hereafters
for your death offered as prize, for

your daunted, youthful smile, for
your determined and unfrocked impudence. I am

sure you will change your attitude. I am very sure
that you will not even love me there, where you are going
and where I, living, shall go. Are you ever sure

of this same thing, this business, this delirious
certainty of aging?

("I am not sure of being close to you, never
totally certain of you, who as a spy
briefs and overcomes me . . . Competition!
life without leashes, entanglements, throat
or impervious freshness. I was delirious and
began to putter to correct
this vice . . . of knowing you armed with wisdom
of knowing you a quarter of a mile away.

As if all the wisdom in the world could
tear dogs apart as I am already doing, as
I will already do, resting in this hut
resting in your pursuit, in the faint

cheer of your dying. Why so much smiling
so much politeness? In the arabesqued smiles

of the wine, flowing and dry, superb the
wine but mixed the mixture!

And I am dead by now next to your shooting
full arrows for my Parmesan cheese, in the
laughter of life and death, entireties and sponges
I have no more to say, just like you who
darts or disappears.)

Amelia Rosselli, 1976

Photograph: Luigi Ghirri. *Reggio Emilia*, 1985

ELZEVIR

In his own way, the salesman is an idealist. More of an idealist than the poet: he's an idealist by trade—in the sense that his profession forces him to extol the praises of a reality which in and of itself is even more naked and sad than that made sublime by the poet's divine breath.

Alberto Savinio, ca. 1930–40

Photograph: George Krause. *La Belva*, Rome, 1977

LIFE IS BETTER THAN DEATH

She confessed she had prayed for her husband's death, and Cesare put down his coffee cup and sat with his butt between his lips, not puffing as she talked.

Armando, Etta said, had fallen in love with a cousin who had come during the summer from Perugia for a job in Rome. Her father had suggested that she live with them, and Armando and Etta, after talking it over, decided to let her stay for a while. They would save her rent to buy a second-hand television set so they could watch "Lascia o Raddoppia," the quiz program that everyone in Rome watched on Thursday nights, and that way save themselves the embarrassment of waiting for invitations and having to accept them from neighbors they didn't like. The cousin came, Laura Ansaldo, a big-boned pretty girl with thick brown hair and large eyes. She slept on the sofa in the living room, was easy to get along with, and made herself helpful in the kitchen before and after supper. Etta had liked her until she noticed that Armando had gone mad over the girl. She then tried to get rid of Laura but Armando threatened he would leave if she bothered her. One day Etta had come home from work and found

(continued on page 134)

Bernard Malamud, 1950

Photograph: Charles Traub. *Marriage on the Rocks*, Naples, 1981

them naked in the marriage bed, engaged in the act. She had screamed and wept. She called Laura a stinking whore and swore she would kill her if she didn't leave the house that minute. Armando was contrite. He promised he would send the girl back to Perugia, and the next day in the Stazione Termini, had put her on the train. But the separation from her was more than he could bear. He grew nervous and miserable. Armando confessed himself one Saturday night, and for the first time in ten years, took communion, but instead of calming down he desired the girl more strongly. After a week he told Etta that he was going to get his cousin and bring her back to Rome.

"If you bring that whore here," Etta shouted, "I'll pray to Christ that you drop dead before you get back."

"In that case," Armando said, "start praying."

When he left the house she fell on her knees and prayed with all her heart for his death.

That night Armando went with a friend to get Laura. The friend had a truck and was going to Assisi. On the way back he would pick them up in Perugia and drive to Rome. They started out when it was still twilight but it soon grew dark. Armando drove for a while, then felt sleepy and crawled into the back of the truck. The Perugian hills were foggy after a hot September day and the truck hit a rock in the road a hard bump. Armando, in deep sleep, rolled out of the open tailgate of the truck, hitting the road with head and shoulders, then rolling down the hill. He was dead before he stopped rolling. When she heard of this Etta fainted away and it was two days before she could speak. After that she had prayed for her own death and often did.

Etta turned her back to the other tables, though they were empty, and wept openly and quietly.

After a while Cesare squashed his butt. "Calma, Signora. If God had wanted your husband to live he would still be living. Prayers have little relevance to the situation. To my way of thinking the whole thing was no more than a co-incidence. It's best not to go too far with religion or it becomes troublesome."

"A prayer is a prayer," she said. "I suffer for mine."

Cesare pursed his lips. "But who can judge these things? They're much more complicated than most of us know. In the case of my wife I didn't pray for her death but I confess I might have wished it. Am I in a better position than you?"

PLEASURES

At Caloria, instead, standing by the slightly ajar high front doors, young men with saffron-colored T-shirts and gold chains and old gentlemen in dark suits and stiff collars stay awake talking about women until the first rooster's crow.

Vitaliano Brancati, 1943

Photograph: Antonio Conti. *Soccer Fan, Rosso-Neri Brigade*, Milan, 1980

ITALIAN SKETCH BOOK

Be it known to you, kind reader, that the social, like the physical atmosphere of Italy, is wonderfully insinuating: one discovers his adaptation at once. The Italians seem to know intuitively the latent points of sympathy between themselves and those with whom they come in contact; a short time serves either to convince them that their acquaintance never can become a friend, or to make him so almost immediately. Nor is this all. Let a genuine Italian discern but the glimmerings of congenial sentiment, and you have his confidence; and if there be aught noble within you, the very alacrity with which you are trusted, will secure it from abuse.

Henry T. Tuckerman, 1848

Photograph: Mario Lasalandra. *Alone*, Padua, ca. 1978

TORREGRECA

They come with their hoes hooked over one shoulder. On the other they carry a bundle of thorny twigs for lighting fires. Some lead donkeys draped with long, pendulous sacks of grass, topped by a load of firewood. Old women amble along, forgetful as the old are of the pair of pigs or sheep they are supposed to be driving. At the bottom of the track, while the animals mill around on the bridge blocking traffic, they will argue about which ones belong to whom. Small boys of ten leading goats on ropes stop at the edge of the road, then whoop down the hill, dragging the balking animals behind them. The old and the young alike have been "out for a stroll" with the animals, and the frivolous amusement implied by the phrase is unfair—for there was no choice. Every member of the family must do something; they were sent out to graze their miniature flocks on the road verges.

Next may come a woman with her mules lead rope wrapped dangerously around her neck to leave her hands free for knitting as she walks. Down at the bridge a husband who wishes to appear the ruler of his destiny, at least in public, makes his wife get down from their donkey and climbs on himself. The wife, robbed of her seat for the only climb of the trip, grabs onto the donkey's tail and allows herself to be dragged the rest of the way home.

Tired and sullen, they "withdraw" from the day, as they say in dialect, and return to the one-room houses they share with donkeys, children, pigs, chickens, in-laws, and, of course, Grandmother. The first thing they do is turn the radio on loud enough to rattle the pots and pans hanging on the walls. This one act symbolizes a return to civilization.

Ann Cornelisen, 1969

Photograph: Mario Giacomelli. *The Good Earth*, Senigallia, 1964–65

PICKWICK'S WISDOM

Collective nouns create confusion. "People, audience. . . ." One day, you'll
realize it is us. And you thought it was them.

Ennio Flaiano, 1956

Photograph: Uliano Lucas. *Demonstration at the Pirelli Works*, Milan, 1977

ROMAN DIARY: ARRIVAL

From the air, the green and deep-chocolate fields make intarsia like the floors of Herculaneum. Then a countryside that has lost its rural pattern to the scrawlings of attack and defense and been left notched with boomerang-shaped trenches and perforated with the craters of shells. Some of the houses still keep their pink roofs, but many are stove-in or broken barnacles. The cattle look as small as lice. Even after you have landed, it is hard to grasp that you have really come to Rome. You are still in the world of the air, as, from the airfield, you watch sturgeon-snouted planes taking off like fish surprised in shallows.

The man who drove me into Rome turned out to come from Massachusetts, and we talked about the cranberry crop on Cape Cod. They had written him that the warm spell in March had brought the cranberries out prematurely, and he was worried for fear a frost would kill them. The freshness of the campagna in the morning, with the donkey-carts going to town, excluded any idea of its antiquity. I asked the driver about some old stumps of Roman ruins—fragments of brown brick masonry, with weeds growing out of them like hairs on warts—and he answered, "I guess that's the old water line." They seemed sordid and completely irrelevant to the beautiful clear spring morning and the familiar-looking American gas station where we stopped to fill up our tank.

Edmund Wilson, 1945

Photograph: Gabriele Basilico. Untitled, from *Portraits of Factories, Milan*, 1980

THAT AWFUL MESS ON VIA MERULANA

The vigorous new forces, then effecting in Italian society that profound renewal, were inspired by the ancient severity or at least by the severe faces of the Lictors, but the renewal also was flavored by their endowment of little clubs (staves tightly bound to the handle of the ax, not only emblematic). Instead of wasting their strength in philosophizing (*primum vivere*), they devoted themselves to paving with the most verbose of good intentions the road to Hell. Gassified into funereal menace, made Word (and Wind), they conspired with great impetus, in that whirlwind of air and dust they stirred up, to kiss the ass even of the clouds, destroying all separation of powers and also the living being generally known as the Fatherland: the distinction of the "three powers," which the great and modest sociologist of the slightly askew wig, observing the best institutions of the Romans and the wisest and more recent of English history, had isolated with such lucidity. Italy's new resurrection followed a not very clothed (as far as the human species was concerned) renaissance, with the pictorial or poetical forms which the world had hailed as indecent and, at the same time, masterful. And this rebirth clung, with an air of bringing it to the best possible conclusion, to a *risorgimento* a little too generous in squeezing pathos from the locks of its troubadours, shaggy or bearded, or generously mustachioed, or glorious in their muttonchops or sideburns, all in any case needing—to our taste—the radical attentions of a Figaro with drastic scissors. The effect that this above-mentioned resurrection extracted from its entrails, ruttingly eager at last to dispose of all the dispositions made disposable by political power, was the effect produced found every time: I mean every time that absolute power is assumed, conglomerating the three controls—discerned by Charles Louis di Secondat di Montesquieu with much clear thinking, in book eleven, chapter six, of his little treatise of roughly eight hundred pages on the *esprit des lois*—conglomerating them, all three, in a single and triply impenetrable and unremovable mafia.

Carlo Emilio Gadda, 1957

Photograph: William Klein. *Palazzo delle Esposizione*, Rome, 1956

GLEANINGS IN EUROPE: ITALY

Strangers are no longer expected to kneel at the appearance of the Host in the streets, or even in the churches. The people understand the prejudices of Protestants, and, unless offensively obtruded, seem disposed to let them enjoy them in peace. I saw a strong proof of this lately:—A friend of mine, walking with myself, stepped aside in a narrow street, for a purpose that often induces men to get into corners. He thought himself quite retired; but, as I stopped for him to rejoin me, a crowd collected around the spot he had just quitted. Without his knowing it, the image of a Madonna was placed in the wall, directly above the spot he had chosen, and of course it had been defiled! I saw all this myself; and it is a proof of the change that exists in this particular, that I dared to remain to watch the result, though my friend himself thought it prudent to retire. A priest appeared, and the wall was sprinkled with holy water, while the people stood looking on, some at the wall and some at me, in grave silence. Thirty years ago such a blunder might have cost us both our lives.

James Fenimore Cooper, 1838

Photograph: Martino Marangoni. *Florence*, 1985

WOMEN AND THE VOTE

Honorable colleages!*

I believe we can conclude the debate this evening, since all points of view have been well presented to the Chamber. However, the subject at hand is so ripe for discussion it is almost rotten. In Italy we have been talking about it for sixty years, and we talk about it today because a bill has been presented so that it will no longer be talked about tomorrow.

My friend Lupi argues that if, for sixty years, ever since Lanza, women have not been given the vote, it is a sign that no problem exists; his argument has no basis.

Let's begin by saying that women's suffrage is neither a question of democracy nor of aristocracy. Would you like some evidence? One of the most democratic countries in the world, and certainly the most democratic in Europe, is Switzerland; yet Switzerland is the only country, together with Italy, that has not yet given women the vote. Now none of you would disagree that Spain is a rigidly Catholic, strongly traditional, chivalric country, having its roots in the family unit; yet, the Spain of De Rivera has universal female suffrage, and no catastrophe has issued from it until now.

Let's not make it a question of north and south, either, seeing the industrial north as for it while the agricultural south is against it. That is not true. For one thing, the majority of the speakers are southerners, yet . . . those who have spoken out against the bill are but two: a Tuscan and a Bolognese (*laughter*).

Let's strip this debate, then, of all but the essential elements. I would like to remind my honorable friend Lupi that we, too, are a major party now. At this point we can no longer set aside the question of universal suffrage. . . . It is not true that this issue has gone unnoticed. Like my friend Lupi, I, too, declare that in my travels I have rarely found a woman who asked for the right to vote. This fact is a tribute to Italian women. . . . But here I have a stack of telegrams from women Fascists—I say women Fascists—who claim this modest right. And on top of the pile is one with a signature that should make you think. It is the signature of Mrs. Pepe, the mother of Ugo Pepe who was assassinated in Milan. The telegram says: "Strong nucleus of women Fascists and the families of Fascists who have died send their support of the vote for women through me." And I could extract from this stack of telegrams names of the individual backers: for example, women Fascists from the province of Caserta, women Fascists from the province of Messina—but I do not want to bore you by reading these telegrams, which indicate what the tendency of the women Fascists's world is.

Now the Honorable Vicini has reminded us that in the Fascist Claims of 1919 regarding the return to origins, this issue of suffrage was completely covered. Let us not get off the track by discussing whether women are superior or in-

Benito Mussolini, 1925

Photograph: Andrea Maurano. *Via Montenapoleone, Milan, 1981*

ferior; we realize that they are different. . . . Do we live perhaps in the Middle Ages, when women were locked inside castles and waited on the balcony for the return of the Crusaders? No. We live in this century: an arid and sad century, if you will, but one we accept because we can change it; it is a century of capitalism, that is to say, of a particular system of social life. And this system of social life, which is already a century old, has torn women from the household hearth, driven them by the millions into factories (*murmurs*) and . . . into offices, and violently inserted them into public life. And, while you may be terrified by the thought that every four years a women might drop her ballot into the ballot box, you are not at all frightened to see female teachers, professors, lawyers, and doctors methodically invading all fields of human activity (*approval*). And they are not doing it, gentlemen, on a whim; they are doing it out of necessity! (*Approval.*) . . . So, you think that all this takes the poetry out of life? No. It gives it another kind of poetry! ("*Bravo*"!) Every century has its own poetry. ("*Yes!*") . . . The new poetry puts life on another level. . . .

Some people think that the extension, the recognition, of this right to vote will cause catastrophes. I deny that. In the long run it has not even provoked men, because out of eleven million citizens who should be exercising their self-styled right, fully six million do not even bother to vote (*approval*). And in certain regions this percentage is even greater; only twenty or seventeen percent bother to vote. The same will happen with women. Maybe only half of them will *ever* exercise their right to vote.

Nothing new will happen in the home for a very simple reason. . . . The life of a woman is always dominated by love, either for her children or for a man. If tomorrow a woman loves her husband, she will vote for him and for his party. If she does not love him, she will vote against him! (*Hysterical laughter.*) . . . Without slipping into feminist exaggerations, which attribute qualities to women that in my opinion they do not possess, I think that in our national society the contribution of female administrative action could prove very useful.

I do not think this law will give rise to waves of suffragettes. First of all, there is our will to militate against it. Second, Italian women have always been discreet. If there were no other reasons for giving them the vote, there would still be this: they have never caused uproars; they have never become upset in a country where there are always those who upset and those who are upset (*laughter and approval*). They have remained calm: they have made their voices heard with great dignity and only when they saw that the question was on the table.

There is no doubt, then, that the place women occupy in society today is vast and is only getting vaster. You cannot drive women back into the positions they held a century or two ago, unless a catastrophe occurs within capitalism and we are reduced to conditions of life we thought we had already surpassed.

Let us put aside the question of war. Women have done great things during the war, and there are examples of superb female heroism . . . But there is something else to be considered, gentlemen: in the unavoidable war of tomorrow (this is a hypothesis of which we must always remind ourselves), the place of women will be even greater. In a bill not yet presented to you (but which will be, in the near future), which has already been passed by the Senate and entitled "Mobilization Law for the Nation at War," female mobilization has been given thorough consideration. Article 3 says:

> In the event of partial or general mobilization, all citizens, men and women, are required to come to the moral and material defense of the nation and be subject to the discipline of war.

Thus we are not talking about prize-giving; we are talking about the simple recognition of a fact that it is not in our power to ignore or even modify.

That is all.

Some people make silly jokes about the attitude of the majority and say: the majority is against it, will talk about it, and will vote as the government and its leader wish. There is nothing funny about this matter. Our strength is in subordination, in accepting discipline, especially when it is unwanted (*applause*), because when it is easy everyone is glad to adapt himself. And remember, that in this subordination of all to the will of a leader, which is not a rash will but a serious and meditative one proven by events, in this subordination Fascism found its strength yesterday, and will find its strength and glory tomorrow (*long, lively applause*).[†]

*The Italian Chamber of Deputies in Rome held a session on May 15, 1925 (from 4 to 6 P.M.), which followed upon a general discussion begun on May 14, on the bill "The Admission of Women to the Administrative Electorate." The following members spoke, in order of appearance: Angelo Manaresi, Egilberto Martire, Ruggero Grieco, Giacomo Acerbo, Dario Lupi (interrupted by Prime Minister Mussolini once). Afterward, the Prime Minister gave the speech reproduced here (from Acts of the Italian Parliament, Chamber of Deputies, Session cited, Legislature cited, vol. 4, pp. 3610–3672).

[†]The general discussion on the bill cited closed with a hand count on the following order of the day, proposed by Deputy Giacomo Acerbo: "The Chamber approves the premises of the bill and passes on to the discussion of its articles" (from Acts of the Italian Parliament, vol. 4, pp. 3632–3633).

TRANSATLANTIC SKETCHES

One may say without injustice to anybody that the state of mind of a great many foreigners in Rome is one of intense impatience for the moment when all other foreigners shall have departed. One may confess to this state of mind, and be no misanthrope. Rome has passed so completely for the winter months into the hands of the barbarians, that that estimable character, the "quiet observer," finds it constantly harder to concentrate his attention. He has an irritating sense of his impressions being perverted and adulterated; the venerable visage of Rome betrays an unbecoming eagerness to see itself mirrored in English, American, German eyes. It is not simply that you are never first or never alone at the classic or historic spots where you have dreamt of persuading the shy *genius loci* into confidential utterance; it is not simply that St. Peter's, the Vatican, the Palatine, are forever ringing with English voices: it is the general oppressive feeling that the city of the soul has become for the time a monstrous mixture of the watering-place and the curiosity-shop, and that its most ardent life is that of the tourists who haggle over false intaglios, and yawn through palaces and temples. But you are told of a happy time when these abuses begin to pass away, when Rome becomes Rome again, and you may have it all to yourself. "You may like Rome more or less now," I was told during the height of the season, "but you must wait till the month of May to love it. Then the foreigners, or the excess of them, are gone; the galleries and ruins are empty, and the place," said my informant, who was a Frenchman, *"renait à elle-même."* Indeed, I was haunted all winter by an irresistible prevision of what Rome *must* be in spring. Certain charming places seem to murmur: "Ah, this is nothing! Come back in May, and see the sky above us almost black with its excess of blue, and the new grass already deep, but still vivid, and the white roses tumbling in odorous spray over the walls, and the warm radiant air dropping gold into all our coloring."

A month ago I spent a week in the country, and on my return, the first time I went into the Corso, I became conscious of a change. Something very pleasant had happened, but at first I was at a loss to define it. Then suddenly I comprehended: there were but half as many people, and these were chiefly good Italians.

Henry James, 1875

Photograph: William Klein. *Red Light*, Rome, 1956

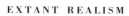

RAMBLES IN ITALY

The moral and intellectual character, particularly of the southern Italian, like that of the savage, is passive; but he is not like the savage roused to action by the impulse only of the animal appetites. Living in a country where there remain so many splendid vestiges of civilized man, and where there exists such a variety of objects to exercise the imagination, and furnish a perpetual source of enjoyment to the most refined taste, his passions and desires have a range as unbounded as the objects of society. The artificial restraints of polished life, operating however with less force upon the Italian, suffer all the natural beauties and deformities of their character to appear.

James Sloan, 1818

Photograph: Franco Zecchin. *Homicide of the Mafioso Stefano Bontate, Palermo*, 1981

THE OLD BRIDGE AT FLORENCE

Taddeo Gaddi built me. I am old
   Five centuries old. I plant my foot of
      stone
   Upon the Arno, as St. Michael's own
   Was planted on the dragon. Fold by
      fold
Beneath me as it struggles, I behold
   Its glistening scales. Twice hath it
      overthrown
   My kindred and companions. Me alone
   It moveth not, but is by me controlled.
I can remember when the Medici
   Were driven from Florence; longer still
      ago
   The final wars of Ghibelline and Guelf.
Florence adorns me with her jewelry;
   And when I think that Michael Angelo
   Hath leaned on me, I glory in myself.

Henry Wadsworth Longfellow, 1889

Photograph: Giorgio Lotti. *Flood Waters of the Arno*, Florence, 1966

THE BELLY OF NAPLES

The Neapolitans are real gluttons for fruit: but they never spend more than a penny at a time. In Naples a penny can buy you six little pears, slightly spoiled, but never mind: can buy you a pound of figs, slightly mushy from the sun: can buy you ten or twelve of those little yellow plums that seem to look feverish: can buy you a bunch of black grapes: can buy you a small, yellow, slightly bruised, slightly rotten melon: from the vendor of watermelons, the red ones, you can get two slices of the ones that have turned out bad, I mean those that are more white than red.

The Neapolitans are also gluttonous for some other things: the *spassatiempo*, that is to say, watermelon or melon seed, oven-baked lima beans and chickpeas; with a penny you can nibble away half the day, the tongue stings, the stomach swells, as if after a real meal.

But the greatest object of gluttony is the *soffritto:* cuts of pork meat cooked in oil, tomato, and red pepper, all hashed together to form a red heap that is beautiful to see and can be served in slices. They cost five cents each and feel like they're going to explode in your mouth.

Matilde Serao, 1906

Photograph: Charles Traub. *Pines and Melons*, Naples, 1982

Resurrected Legends IS DEVOTED TO THE PROTEAN QUALITY of the Italian myth. Necessity curtails movement to new frontiers. As a result there is no expanding of the Italian imagination except as it digs into its own layered archaeology. Inspired by a tradition of using existing materials anew, the excavation is not a search for utopia: the dream of otherness never really disturbs the active sleep of the Italian night. The myth is whole when it awakens each morning.

THE INNOCENTS ABROAD

I wish to say one word about Michael Angelo Buonarotti. I used to worship the mighty genius of Michael Angelo—that man who was great in poetry, painting, sculpture, architecture—great in every thing he undertook. But I do not want Michael Angelo for breakfast—for luncheon—for dinner—for tea— for supper—for between meals. I like a change, occasionally. In Genoa, he designed every thing; in Milan he or his pupils designed every thing; he designed the Lake of Como; in Padua, Verona, Venice, Bologna, who did we ever hear of from guides, but Michael Angelo? In Florence, he painted every thing, designed every thing, nearly, and what he did not design he used to sit on a favorite stone and look at, and they showed us the stone. In Pisa he designed every thing but the old shot-tower, and they would have attributed that to him if it had not been so awfully out of the perpendicular. He designed the piers of Leghorn and the customhouse regulations of Civita Vecchia. But, here—here it is frightful. He designed St. Peter's; he designed the Pope; he designed the Pantheon, the uniform of the Pope's soldiers, the Tiber, the Vatican, the Coliseum, the Capitol, the Tarpeian Rock, the Barberini Palace, St. John Lateran, the Campagna, the Appian Way, the Seven Hills, the Baths of Caracalla, the Claudian Aqueduct, the Cloaca Maxima—the eternal bore designed the Eternal City, and unless all men and books do lie, he painted every thing in it! Dan said the other day to the guide, "Enough, enough, enough! Say no more! Lump the whole thing! say that the Creator made Italy from designs by Michael Angelo!"

I never felt so fervently thankful, so soothed, so tranquil, so filled with a blessed peace, as I did yesterday when I learned that Michael Angelo was dead.

Mark Twain, 1869

Photograph: Cuchi White. *Palazzo Reale*, Genoa, ca. 1980

NOTES ON ITALY

Neither Rome nor Florence, nor any other city of Italy, possesses a school of painting. Their academies teach nothing but drawing, which is, indeed, exquisitely fine, and productive of the most beautiful engravings; but painting is learned without any established practice, or in vicious imitation of that which is erroneous. There is not even a good or honest colorman in Rome or Florence, and artists use, without system, pigments of which they know not the true names. The best painters in Italy are foreigners, who more eagerly seize upon the excellences they have come so far to study; and without them the art would be in danger of being totally lost where it has so gloriously flourished.

In regard to the peculiar excellencies which certain painters of past time have shown in their works, nothing has more puzzled the professors and critics of art. It has appeared to me that although a great deal must have depended upon the capacity of the artist and his means of information, and a vast deal on the nature of his employment and encouragement, almost as much advantage has been derived from accidental circumstances. The Italians, who enjoy a clear sky, and witness in their sun-sets the most glowing colors, are surprised that the Hollanders, living in an atmosphere of gray mist, should have produced so many excellent colorists. I conceive it to have arisen chiefly from the circumstance that they were so. A vapory atmosphere, that reduces all colors at a distance to one hue of gray, serves, at the same time, to render every color which is near, not only more distinct, but more agreeably illuminated; but, under a blue sky the shadows are necessarily tinged with blue, and the eye becoming accustomed to vivid colors, too easily rests satisfied with the most violent contrasts, both in nature and the works of art.

The atmosphere of England, in like manner, has contributed to produce a good taste in coloring which was confirmed by the example and authority of Reynolds, who so well understood the principles of the Flemish masters. Giorgione, Titian and Paul Veronese were, it is true, Italians, and rank at the head of good colorists; but the situation of Venice, built in the water, essentially softens its atmosphere and combines the advantages of Holland and Italy. The happy genius of Coreggio derived his theory of light and color certainly not from his visit to Rome.

Rembrandt Peale, 1831

Photograph: Mitch Epstein. *Venice*, 1977

ITALIAN ITINERARY

Places like these are everywhere in the ancient world: hiding places, *lustri*, recesses, caverns. And I like to imagine the ancients, to whom distances, even the most familiar ones, seem to be enormous, as children to whom the corners within their own domestic walls seem to be something to explore or to leave unexplored; they repair to them in their hours of dream and fantasy, even thinking they are invisible if they hide under a table. No differently did ancient men, and even primitive men today, see the distances separating them from certain places of the earth; both of them, ancient as well as primitive, were sedentary not only because of their slow means of transport, but because, moving only if need forced them to, they were hardly accustomed to traveling. Above all, however, it is the childlike love of hiding places that draws the ancients and the primitives together—and the fact that they both avoid certain paths because of the aura exuding from shrubs and caves along the way. Beyond the horizon that the eye could see, they posited a fable. You only have to hear how in many places in the Orient and the Mediterranean people still fantasize about distant places and, on the other hand, how mysterious they consider travelers, pilgrims, and shepherds, people who do cross great distances.

Corrado Alvaro, 1941

Photograph: Jerry Gordon. *Sistine Chapel*, Rome, 1983

JOURNAL OF A VISIT TO EUROPE AND THE LEVANT

On these still summer days the fair Venetians float about in full bloom like pond lilies—Grand Canal not straight and stiff but irregular with projections for advantageous fronts. . . . You, at first, think it a freshet; it will subside, not permanent, —only a temporary condition of things.—St. Mark's at sunset, gilt mosaics, pinnacles, looks like holyday affair. As if the Grand Turk had pitched his pavilion here for a summer's day. 800 years! Inside the precious marbles, from extreme age, look like a mural of rare old soaps.—Have an unctuous look. Fairly steamed with old devotions as refectories with old dinners.—In Venice nothing to see for the Venetian.—Rather be in Venice on rainy day, than in other capital on fine one.—My guide. How I met him, & where. Lost his money in 1848 Revolution & by traveling.—Today in one city, tomorrow in next. Fine thing to travel. When rich, plenty compliment.

How you do, Antonio—hope you very well, Antonio—Now Antonio no money, Antonio no compliment. Get out of de way Antonio. Go to the devil, Antonio. Antonio you go shake yourself. You know dat Sir, dat to de rich man, de poor man habe always de bad smell? You know dat Sir? (For Con. Man)

Yes, Antonio, I am not unaware of that. Charitably disposed. Old blind man, give something & God will bless you (Will give, but doubt the blessing.) (Antonio good character for Con. Man) Did not want to die. Heaven. You believe dat? I go dere, see how I like it first.—His rich anecdote. Byron swimming over by (secrecy) to wake a lady in palace opposite.

Herman Melville, ca. 1856

Photograph: Gianni Berengo Gardin. *Venice*, 1984

NOTES OF TRAVEL

We afterwards went into the sculpture gallery, where I looked at the Faun of Praxiteles, and was sensible of a peculiar charm in it; a sylvan beauty and homeliness, friendly and wild at once. The lengthened, but not preposterous ears, and the little tail, which we infer, have an exquisite effect, and make the spectator smile in his very heart. This race of fauns was the most delightful of all that antiquity imagined. It seems to me that a story, with all sorts of fun and pathos in it, might be contrived on the idea of their species having become intermingled with the human race; a family with the faun blood in them having prolonged itself from the classic era till our own days. The tail might have disappeared, by dint of constant intermarriages with ordinary mortals; but the pretty hairy ears should occasionally reappear in members of the family; and the moral instincts and intellectual characteristics of the faun might be most picturesquely brought out, without detriment to the human interest of the story. Fancy this combination in the person of a young lady!

Nathaniel Hawthorne, ca. 1855

Photograph: Charles Traub. *Madonna of the Wristwatch*, Rome, 1981

THE SALAMANDER

To the foreigner, we look like characters out of an opera, exaggerated and larger than life. The reverse is true. The opera is only a pale shadow of our history.

Morris West, 1973

Photograph: Gabriele Basilico. Untitled, Milan, ca. 1980

GLEANINGS OF EUROPE: ITALY

I know too little of Italian society to say anything new about it, or even to speak very confidently on any of the old usages. The daughters of particular families, I believe, are getting to have more of a voice in the choice of husbands than formerly; though France is still much in advance of Italy in this respect. I take this one fact to be the touchstone of domestic manners; for the woman who has freely made her own selection will hesitate long before she consents to destroy the great pledge of connubial affection. *Cicisbeism* certainly exists, for I have seen proofs of it; but I incline to the opinion that foreigners do not exactly understand the custom. By what I can learn, too, it is gradually yielding to the opinions of the age. A foreigner married to an Italian of rank, and who has long been resident in Italy, tells me its social tone is greatly impaired by the habits of the women, who are so much disposed to devote themselves to their sentiment in favour of particular individuals, as to have no wish to mingle in general society. Whether these individuals were the husbands or not, the lady did not appear to think it necessary to say.

James Fenimore Cooper, 1838

Photograph: Carla Cerati. *Cocktail Party*, Rome, 1972

EUROPEAN ACQUAINTANCE

I consider the Italian women in general as not only among the handsomest in the world, but as morally admirable for true feminine nature. They possess, in an uncommon completeness, all the elements of perfect womanliness: they are affectionate, constant, unsuspicious, gentle-hearted, almost never coquettish, and have that sweet timidity which we love in women. I say that nature has endowed them with these charming qualities; I do not say that they always keep them undesecrated by vices. But if they are often false to themselves and to others, who most deserves the blame? Women are everywhere very much what men make them; and if the husbands of Italy find their wives unfaithful, it is but the chastisement of their own libertinage. What astonishes one is the ever renewed confidence which the *Italiana* puts in her deceivers, after having been duped again and again. The last lover was a faithless monster, but the new one is sincere and adorable. There is no skepticism in her heart; she has an affectionate trustfulness that is beautiful. "Our women are very credulous," said a Palermitano to me; "tell them you love them, and they believe you immediately."

J. W. De Forest, 1858

Photograph: Mario de Biasi. *Italians Watching*, Milan, 1954

THE THREE CRONES

There were once three sisters who were all young. One was sixty-seven, another seventy-five, and the third ninety-four. Now these girls had a house with a nice little balcony, in the very middle of which was a hole for looking down on people passing along the street. The ninety-four-year-old sister, seeing a handsome young man approach, grabbed her finest scented handkerchief and sent it floating to the street just as the youth passed under the balcony. He picked it up, noticed the delightful scent, and concluded, "It can only belong to a very beautiful maiden." He walked on a way, then came back and rang the doorbell of that house. One of the three sisters answered the door, and the young man asked, "Would you please tell me if a young lady lives in this mansion, by chance?"

"Yes, indeed, and not just one."

"Would you do me a favor and allow me to see the one who lost this handkerchief?"

"No, that is impossible. A girl can't be seen before she's married. That's the rule at our mansion."

The youth was already so thrilled just imagining the girl's beauty that he said, "That's not asking a bit too much. I'll marry her sight unseen. Now I'm going to tell my mother I've found a lovely maiden whom I intend to marry."

He went home and told his mother all about it. She said, "Dear son, take care and don't let those people trick you. You must think before you act."

"They're not asking a bit too much. I've given my word, and a king must keep his promise," said the young man, who happened to be a king.

He returned to the bride's house and rang the doorbell. The same crone answered the door, and he asked, "Are you her grandmother?"

"That's right, I'm her grandmother."

"Since you're her grandmother, do me a favor and show me at least a finger of the girl."

"No, not now. You'll have to come back tomorrow."

The youth said goodbye and left. As soon as he was gone, the crones made an artificial finger out of the finger of a glove and a false fingernail. In the meantime his eagerness to see the finger kept him awake all night long. The sun came up at last, and he dressed and ran to the house.

"Madam," he said to the crone, "I've come to see my bride's finger."

"Yes, yes," she replied, "right away. You'll see it through the keyhole of this door."

The bride pushed the false finger through the keyhole. Bewitched by its beauty, the young man kissed the finger and slipped a diamond ring onto it. Head over heels in love by then, he said to the crone, "I must marry her forthwith, Granny; I can't wait any longer."

"You can marry her tomorrow, if you like."

"Perfect! I'll marry her tomorrow, on my honor as a king!"

Being rich, the three old women were able to get everything ready overnight for the wedding, down to the tiniest detail. The next day the bride dressed with the help of her two little sisters. The king arrived and said, "I'm here, Granny."

'Wait a minute, and we'll bring her to you."

Here she came at last, arm in arm with her sisters and covered with seven

Italo Calvino, 1956

Photograph: Douglas Baz. *Sicily*, 1981

veils. "Remember," said the sisters, "you may not look at her face until you are in the bridal chamber."

They went to the church and got married. Afterward the king wanted them all to go to dinner, but the crones would not allow it. "The bride, mind you, isn't used to such foolishness." So the king had to keep quiet. He was dying for night to come when he could be alone with the bride. The crones finally took her to her room, but made him wait outside while they undressed her and put her to bed. At last he went in and found the bride under the covers and two old sisters still busying about the room. He undressed, and the old women went off with the lamp. But he'd brought along a candle in his pocket. He got it, lit it, and what should he see but an old withered crone streaked with wrinkles!

For an instant he was speechless and paralyzed with fright. Then in a fit of rage he seized his wife and hurled her through the window.

Under the window was a vine-covered trellis. The old crone went crashing through the trellis, but the hem of her nightgown caught on a broken slat and held her dangling in the air.

That night three fairies happened to be strolling through the gardens. Passing under the trellis, they spied the dangling crone. At that unexpected sight, all three fairies burst out laughing and laughed until their sides hurt. But when they had laughed their fill, one of them said, "Now that we've had such a good laugh at her expense, we must reward her."

"Indeed we must," agreed another. "I will that you become the most beautiful maiden in the world."

"I will," said the second fairy, "that you have the most handsome of husbands and that he love you with his whole heart."

"I will," said the third fairy, "that you be a great noble lady your whole life long."

At that, the fairies moved on.

At dawn the king awakened and remembered everything. To make sure it wasn't just a bad dream, he opened the window in order to see the monster he'd thrown out the night before. But there on the trellis sat the loveliest of maidens! He put his hands to his head.

"Goodness me, what have I done!" He had no idea how to draw her up, but finally took a sheet off the bed, threw her an end to grab hold of, then pulled her up into the room. Overjoyed to have her beside him once more, he begged her to forgive him, which she did, and they became the best of friends.

In a little while a knock was heard on the door. "It must be Granny," said the king. "Come in, come in!"

The old woman entered and saw in bed, in place of her ninety-four-year-old sister, the loveliest of young ladies, who said, as though nothing were amiss, "Clementine, bring me my coffee."

The old crone put a hand over her mouth to stifle a cry of amazement. Pretending everything was just as it should be, she went off and got the coffee. But the minute the king left the house to attend to his business, she ran to his wife and asked, "How in the world did you become so young?"

"Shhhh!" cautioned the wife. "Lower your voice, please! Just wait until you hear what I did! I had myself planed!"

"Planed! Planed? Who did it for you? I'm going to get planed too."

"The carpenter!"

The old woman went running to the carpenter's shop lickety-split. "Carpenter, will you give me a good planing?"

"Oh, my goodness!" exclaimed the carpenter. "You're already deadwood, but if I plane you, you'll go to kingdom come."

"Don't give it a thought."

"What do you mean, not give it a thought? After I've killed you, what then?"

"Don't worry, I tell you. Here's a thaler."

When he heard "thaler," the carpenter changed his mind. He took the money and said, "Lie down here on my workbench, and I'll plane you all you like," and he proceeded to plane a jaw.

The crone let out a scream.

"Now, now! If you scream, we won't get a thing done."

She rolled over, and the carpenter planed the other jaw. The old crone screamed no more: she was dead as dead can be.

Nothing more was ever heard of the other crone. Whether she drowned, had her throat slit, died in bed or elsewhere, no one knows.

The bride was the only one left in the house with the young king, and they lived happily ever after.

THE STONES OF FLORENCE

The idea of a secret, such as the oil process, which men would murder for, seems to connect painting even more closely with witchcraft. Conflicting accounts are still given of how the oil process came to Italy and was disseminated. Naive authors write about it as if it were some magic concoction or philter guaranteed to give charm or, better, fascination to a painting. Painters were enrolled in the guild of the *Speziali*, or Pharmacists; this was because, like the druggists, they compounded pigments or powders, according to secret formulas, out of imported "spices." With the discovery of perspective, itself a wizard science of numbers, painting, especially in Florence, where everything was pushed to extremes, became more and more a black art. Geniuses like Uccello and Piero della Francesca, who abandoned themselves to perspective studies, neglected their work for the sake of this fata morgana. Piero, who was trained in Florence under Domenico Veneziano, gave the later years of his life to writing mathematical treatises. Like Uccello, he died obscure and neglected—in the little town of Borgo San Sepolcro, where he was born. He, too, had been bewitched by *mazzocchi*, by chalices, cups and cones. . . . Painting was becoming a sweet language.

What happened during the fifteenth century, the age of discovery, in Florentine painting had the character sometimes of a Promethean, sometimes of a Faustian myth. Since the ancient Greeks, no people had been as speculative as the Florentines, and the price of this speculation was heavy. Continual experiments in politics had caused a breakdown of government, as in Athens, and artistic experiment had begun to unhinge the artists. "Ah, Paolo," Donatello is supposed to have remonstrated, "this perspective of yours is making you abandon the certain for the uncertain." The advances in knowledge gave rise to an increase in doubt. By a cunning legerdemain, it was found, a flat surface could be made to appear round.

Mary McCarthy, 1959

Photograph: Gianni Berengo Gardin. *Tuscany*, 1970

AESTHETICS

For example, some will say of two pictures—one without inspiration, in which the author has copied natural objects without intelligence; the other inspired, but without close relation to existing objects—that the first is *realistic*, the second *symbolic*. Others, on the contrary, utter the word *realistic* before a picture strongly felt representing a scene of ordinary life, while they apply that of *symbolic* to another picture that is but a cold allegory. It is evident that in the first case symbolic means artistic and realistic inartistic, while in the second, realistic is synonymous with artistic and symbolic with inartistic. What wonder, then, that some hotly maintain the true art form is the symbolic, and that the realistic is inartistic; others, that the realistic is artistic and the symbolic inartistic? We cannot but grant that both are right, since each uses the same words in such a different sense.

The great disputes about *classicism* and *romanticism* were frequently based upon such equivocations. Sometimes the former was understood as the artistically perfect, and the second as lacking balance and imperfect; at others "classic" meant cold and artificial, "romantic" pure, warm, powerful, truly expressive. Thus it was always possible reasonably to take the side of the classic against the romantic, or of the romantic against the classic. `

Benedetto Croce, 1901

Photograph: Allan Chasanoff. *Mixing It Up*, Florence, 1982

ON MIRACLES

A source of surprise for the foreigner is the frequence with which [the Italians] call for miracles. They call for them all the time and for the smallest problem. What is even more surprising is the great number of miracles that actually occur, some of them even on fixed dates and in established places. Down there, miracles are daily events; everyone blindly relies on them. In Rome, and even more so in the cities of the South, miracles are the only regularly scheduled activities. Streetcars don't run, offices are always closed, telephones make mistakes, trains are prone to collisions; miracles, instead, are perfect. The outcome is that common folks put enormous trust in the supernatural and nourish an invincible distrust for anything that is man-made. Even those most in tune with science and logic grow accustomed to expecting from metaphysics those benefits denied to them by mechanical progress.

Ennio Flaiano, 1956

Photograph: Uliano Lucas. *Naples*, ca. 1977

ROMAN PROMENADE

And so we think back to the word of the great popes of antiquity, frightful evidence of what Rome must have been at the time of Alaric and Byzantium: a land good for sheep, a cave for a few stranded, frightened famine-stricken people, pale with the terror of God's scourges; and possibly even more astonishing, remnants of centuries of mixed blood.

Riccardo Bacchelli, 1962

Photograph: Ferdinando Scianna. *Sotto il Monte: Birthplace of Pope John XXIII*, 1983

THE PASSIONATE SIGHTSEER

The traffic in the streets is frightening for one so little used to going into town. I generally arrive by car at my destination in a panic and am relieved if the driver can manage to stop without my having to cross a street. Maybe late at night or in the first morning hours one could still indulge in such old-fashioned pursuits as sauntering along, stopping in the middle of the street to stare up at facades of palaces and churches.

Bernard Berenson, 1956

Photograph: George Tatge. *Etruscan Gate*, Perugia, 1983

WILLIAM WETMORE STORY AND HIS FRIENDS

The page here, for instance, is Mrs. Story's, who journalises with spirit. "In January one evening came the Cranches, and we sat over the fire and told stories, escaping, I believe, all dangerous topics, such as homeopathy and the respective attractions of New York and Boston." One longs for the "stories" that circulated in this conscious avoidance, and wonders whether they made them up as they went along, or plucked them, by the Florentine fire, as fine flowers of experience. The special experience of the Cranches, that comes back to me from later, from Parisian and other days, on lines of its own, bringing with it the conception of the somewhat melancholy blossom it might have yielded. Memory turns to *them*, indeed, as to precursors of the purest water, whose portion was ever to tread the path rather than to arrive at the goal. Christopher Pearse Cranch, painter, poet, musician, mild and melancholy humorist, produced pictures that the American traveler sometimes acquired and left verses that the American compiler sometimes includes. Pictures and verses had alike, in any case, the mark of his great, his refined personal modesty; it was not in them at least, for good or for ill, to emphasize or insist. That was naturally—as always in such connections—much more the part of his graceful and clever companion, who would have painted, played and written with more effect than he, had her hand been formed for the various implements. There were those, in the general company we are considering (as one now imagines or recalls them), who didn't "go home," and there were those who did; there were those who wouldn't even if they could, and there were those who couldn't even if they would. Each of these classes still shines for me, thus late in the day, with its special colored light, but the light that is softest and kindest, that most poetically veils all plain particulars, hangs over the group last mentioned. Some were not to come home, we make out, till after death; they must have done so—those who had most wanted it—then. The Cranches came before, well before; which gave them but the longer time to be sorry. Then they could sit by New England fires and tell stories, *not* made up, to good purpose. For there were precursors, in those days, in the path of regret, one might even say of repentance, quite as in the path of curiosity and cheer. There were experiments, all round, in every kind of nostalgia, and those only, I daresay, who quite escaped the disease were those who either never "went" at all, or never came back.

Henry James, 1903

Photograph: Carlo Uva. *American*, Venice, 1984

Eternal Charms BEARS THE SIGNATURE OF THE TERRA firma and of Italian daily life. As the faces of a spinning coin are indistinguishable, so here fact and metaphor mingle in the same utterance. This trait permeates Italian discourse and paves the way between museum and street. Along this paradoxical path sculptures are unearthed and mannequins stroll, wearing garments that bare the body in unequivocal testimony to the style of this culture.

MAYBE SOME MORNING

Maybe some morning, walking in a dry air of glass
I shall turn around and see the miracle fulfilled:
With the terror of some drunk, the emptiness
At my shoulders and the void behind me.

Then, as if on a screen, trees, houses,
Hills, thrown together in the usual deception.
But it will be too late. And I will go more silently
With my secret among the men who do not turn.

Eugenio Montale, ca. 1925

Photograph: Roy Gumpel. *Vista through a Stone Window*, Umbria, 1983

FIRESIDE TRAVELS

After dinner, as we sat smoking our pipes on the piazza, our good hostess brought her little daughter, and made her repeat verses utterly unintelligible, but conjecturally moral, and certainly depressing. Once set agoing, she ran down like an alarm-clock. We awaited her subsidence as that of a shower or other inevitable natural phenomenon. More refreshing was the talk of a tall returned Californian, who told us, among other things, that "he shouldn't mind Panahmy's bein' sunk, ollers providin' there **warn't** none of our folks onto it when it went down!"

Our landlady's exhibition of her daughter puts me in mind of something similar, yet oddly different, which happened to Storg and me at Palestrina. We happened to praise the beauty of our stout *locandiera's* little girl. "Ah, she is nothing to her elder sister just married," said the mother. "If you could see her! She is bella, bella, bella!" We thought no more of it; but after dinner, the good creature, with no warning but a tap at the door and a humble *con permesso*, brought her in all her bravery, and showed her off to us as simply and naturally as if she had been a picture. The girl, who was both beautiful and modest, bore it with the dignified aplomb of a statue. She knew we admired her, and liked it, but with the indifference of a rose.

James Russell Lowell, 1864

Photograph: Marcia Lippman. *Viareggio, Tuscany,* 1987

THE STONES OF FLORENCE

There is nothing quite so rich in Florence as the pergamo of dancing putti that was made by Michelozzo and Donatello together for the Prato Duomo. This pergamo is a covered pulpit affixed to an outside corner of the black-and-white-striped Cathedral; from it, on certain feast days, a girdle, said to be the Madonna's, is shown to the people in the piazza below. The story of how the girdle came to Prato is told in fresco inside the Duomo in a reliquary chapel painted by Agnolo Gaddi, one of the Gothic painters of the Trecento. The Madonna, at the time of her Assumption, threw her girdle to St. Thomas, who was standing, with the other Apostles, watching her disappear into the sky. The Apostle, when his time came, entrusted it to an old priest, whose daughter, Maria, fell in love with a Pratese, Michael Dagomari, who had come to the Holy Land as a crusader and remained as a merchant. After a fortunate sea voyage, the pair arrived in Prato, bringing the girdle as the girl's dowry, locked in a little hamper of rushes. Michelozzo's and Donatello's balcony, constructed for the exposition of this relic, is an almost Oriental fantasy; the tall nutmeg-colored baldaquin, carved as if in supple leather, is sustained by a single central column, so that it looks like a graceful umbrella raised over some khan or shah; below is a marble frieze of reveling children, which, by contrast, seems a page from a classic epithalamium. This pure Renaissance work, by the very profusion and order of its details—pilaster, cornice, corbels, single bronze capital—harmonizes in an extraordinary way with the rich, half-Oriental Pisan Romanesque of the facade and long striped flank of the Cathedral, and harmonizes, too, with the fabulous tale of the girdle, the Prato trader in the Holy Land, and the Eastern priest's daughter. The Florentines themselves, Burckhardt noted, were rather indifferent to relics; this no doubt was due less to skepticism than to a dislike of the atmosphere of costly ostentation that always surrounds the cult of old bones and bits of material. Nevertheless, in 1312, a Pratese had the idea of stealing the sacred girdle and selling it to the Florentines; he was put to death, and a reliquary chapel was built to protect it.

This is one of the rare Church legends that centers around a love story, in fact, around an elopement (for the pair ran away from the old priest, who disapproved of their love), and the cult of the Holy Girdle, perhaps for this reason, is very popular in Tuscany.

Mary McCarthy, 1959

Photograph: Roy Gumpel. *Couple in the Street*, 1983

THE EDUCATION OF HENRY ADAMS

For the rest, Italy was mostly an emotion and the emotion naturally centered in Rome. The American parent, curiously enough, while bitterly hostile to Paris, seemed rather disposed to accept Rome as legitimate education, though abused; but to young men seeking education in a serious spirit, taking for granted that everything had a cause, and that nature tended to an end, Rome was altogether the most violent vice in the world, and Rome before 1870 was seductive beyond resistance. The month of May, 1860, was divine. No doubt other young men, and occasionally young women, have passed the month of May in Rome since then, and conceive that the charm continues to exist. Possibly it does—in them—but in 1860 the lights and shadows were still medieval, and medieval Rome was alive; the shadows breathed and glossed, full of soft forms felt by lost senses. No sand-blast of science had yet skinned off the epidermis of history, thought, and feeling. The pictures were uncleaned, the churches unrestored, the ruins unexcavated. Medieval Rome was sorcery. Rome was the worst spot on earth to teach nineteenth-century youth what to do with a twentieth-century world. One's emotions in Rome were one's private affair, like one's glass of absinthe before dinner in the Palais Royal; they must be hurtful, else they could not have been so intense; and they were surely immoral, for no one, priest or politician, could honestly read in the ruins of Rome any other certain lesson than that they were evidence of the just judgments of an outraged God against all the doings of man. This moral unfitted young men for every sort of useful activity; it made Rome a gospel of anarchy and vice; the last place under the sun for educating the young; yet it was, by common consent, the only spot that the young—of either sex and every race—passionately, perversely, wickedly loved.

(continued on page 206)

Henry Adams, 1906

Photograph: Mimmo Jodice. *Museo Nazionale*, Naples, 1980

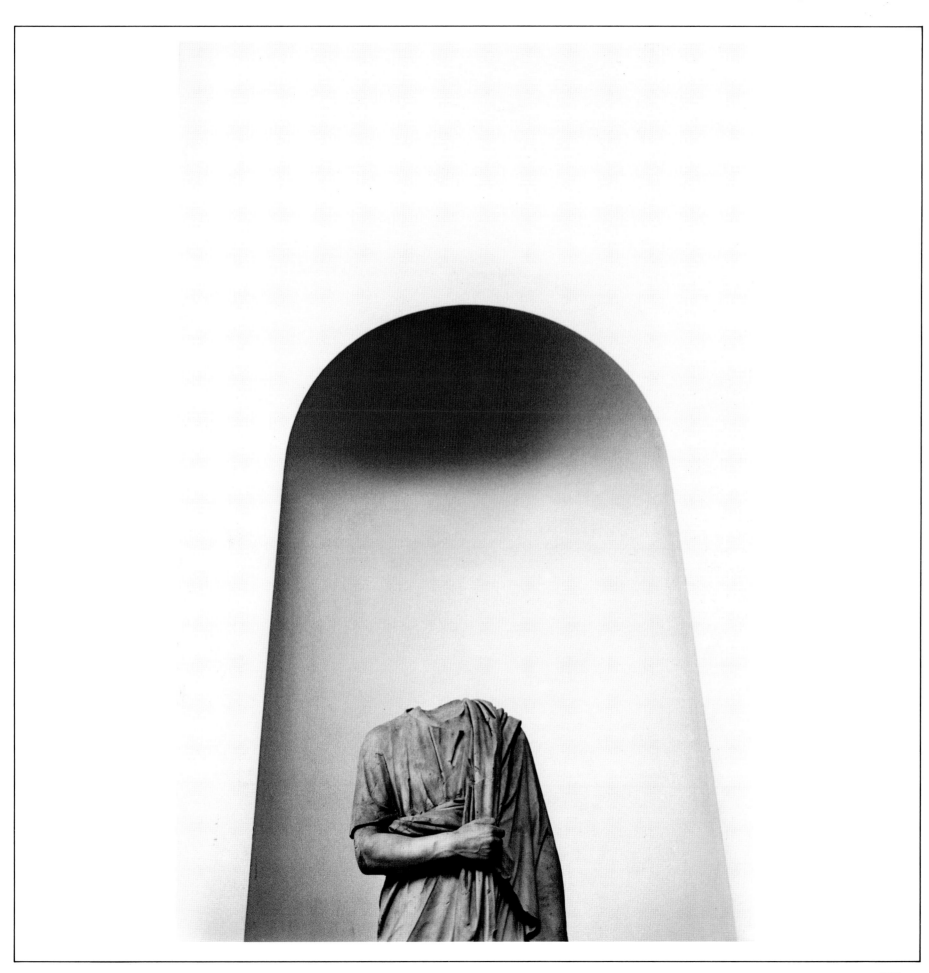

Boys never see a conclusion; only on the edge of the grave can man conclude anything; but the first impulse given to the boy is apt to lead or drive him for the rest of his life into conclusion after conclusion that he never dreamed of reaching. One looked idly enough at the Forum or at St. Peter's, but one never forgot the look, and it never ceased reacting. To a young Bostonian, fresh from Germany, Rome seemed a pure emotion, quite free from economic or actual values, and he could not in reason or common sense foresee that it was mechanically piling up conundrum after conundrum in his educational path, which seemed unconnected but that he had got to connect; that seemed insoluble but had got to be somehow solved. Rome was not a beetle to be dissected and dropped; not a bad French novel to be read in a railway train and thrown out of the window after other bad French novels, the morals of which could never approach the immorality of Roman history. Rome was actual; it was England; it was going to be America. Rome could not be fitted into an orderly, middle-class, Bostonian, systematic scheme of evolution. No law of progress applied to it. Not even time sequences—the last refuge of helpless historians—had value for it. The Forum no more led to the Vatican than the Vatican to the Forum. Rienzi, Garibaldi, Tiberius Gracchus, Aurelian might be mixed up in any relation of time, along with a thousand more, and never lead to a sequence. The great word Evolution had not yet, in 1860, made a new religion of history, but the old religion had preached the same doctrine for a thousand years without finding in the entire history of Rome anything but flat contradiction.

Of course both priests and evolutionists bitterly denied this heresy, but what they affirmed or denied in 1860 had very little importance indeed for 1880. Anarchy lost no ground meanwhile. The problem became only the more fascinating. Probably it was more vital in May, 1860, than it had been in October, 1764, when the idea of writing the Decline and Fall of the city first started, to the mind of Gibbon, "in the close of the evening, as I sat musing in the Church of the Zoccolanti or Franciscan Friars, while they were singing Vespers in the Temple of Jupiter, on the ruins of the Capitol." Murray's Handbook had the grace to quote this passage from Gibbon's *Autobiography*, which led Adams more than once to sit at sunset on the steps of the Church of Santa Maria di Ara Coeli, curiously wondering that not an inch had been gained by Gibbon— or all the historians since—toward explaining the Fall. The mystery remained unsolved; the charm remained intact. Two great experiments of Western civilization had left there the chief monuments of their failure, and nothing proved that the city might not still survive to express the failure of a third.

THE SMILE OF ITALY

In Italy one learns how to smile at time: perhaps not to get intoxicated by it. A race of builders has rooted itself in a land of earthquakes; the most sensitive people in the hands of the most unavoidable of all histories has entrusted its destiny to costume, language, taste, whims, and wits: ephemeral glories; . . . unplacated and wondering life has found in these fragile banks the most efficacious and discreet reasons to pause. When and where it draws away, it does so with great self-constraint, at a quiet pace, keeping wisely alert. It recedes before time without confusion and without fear.

Riccardo Bacchelli, 1962

Photograph: Cuchi White. *Villa Farnesina*, Rome, ca. 1980

TO AN OLD PHILOSOPHER IN ROME

(for George Santayana)

On the threshold of heaven, the figures in the street
Become the figures of heaven, the majestic movement
Of men growing small in the distances of space,
Singing, with smaller and still smaller sound,
Unintelligible absolution and an end—

The threshold, Rome, and that more merciful Rome
Beyond, the two alike in the make of the mind.
It is as if in a human dignity
Two parallels become one, a perspective, of which
Men are part both in the inch and in the mile.

How easily the blown banners change to wings . . .
Things dark on the horizons of perception,
Become accompaniments of fortune, but
Of the fortune of the spirit, beyond the eye,
Not of its sphere, and yet not far beyond.

The human end in the spirit's greatest reach,
The extreme of the known in the presence of the extreme
Of the unknown.

Wallace Stevens, 1952

Photograph: Linda Hackett. *Lesson at the E. Cecchetti School of Classical Dance*, Capri, 1982

BEYOND THE ALPS

(On the train from Rome to Paris. 1950, the year Pius XII
defined the dogma of Mary's bodily Assumption.)

Reading how even the Swiss had thrown the sponge
in once again and Everest was still
unscaled, I watched our Paris Pullman lunge
mooning across the fallow Alpine snow.
O bella Roma! I saw our stewards go
forward on tiptoe banging on their gongs.
Life changed to landscape. Much against my will
I left the City of God where it belongs.
There the skirt-mad Mussolini unfurled
the eagle of Caesar. He was one of us
only, pure prose. I envy the conspicuous
waste of our grandparents on their Grand Tours—
long-haired Victorian sages bought the universe,
while breezing on their trust funds through the world.

When the Vatican made Mary's Assumption dogma,
the crowds at San Pietro screamed *Papa.*
The Holy Father dropped his shaving glass,
and listened. His electric razor purred,
his pet canary chirped on his left hand.
The lights of science couldn't hold a candle
to Mary risen—at one miraculous stroke,
angel-wing'd, gorgeous as a jungle bird!
But who believed this? Who could understand?
Pilgrims still kissed St. Peter's brazen sandal.
The Duce's lynched, bare, booted skull still spoke.
God herded his people to the *coup de grâce*—
the costumed Switzers sloped their pikes to push,
O Pius, through the monstrous human crush. . . .

Our mountain-climbing train had come to earth.
Tired of the querulous hush-hush of the wheels,
the blear-eyed ego kicking in my berth
lay still, and saw Apollo plant his heels
on terra firma through the morning's thigh . . .
each backward, wasted Alp, a Parthenon,
fire-branded socket of the Cyclops's eye.
There were no tickets for that altitude
once held by Hellas, when the Goddess stood,
prince, pope, philosopher and golden bough,
pure mind and murder at the scything prow—
Minerva, the miscarriage of the brain.

Now Paris, our black classic, breaking up
like killer kings on an Etruscan cup.

Robert Lowell, 1950

Photograph: Luigi Ghirri. *Alpe di Siusi,* 1979

ROME

Just as foretold, it all was there.
Bone china columns gently fluted
Among the cypress groves, and the reputed
Clarity of the air,

There was the sun-bleached skeleton
Of History with all its sins
Withered away, the slaves and citizens
Mercifully undone.

With here and there an armature
Of iron or a wall of brick,
It lay in unhistoric peace, a trick
Of that contrived, secure

Arrested pterodactyl flight
Inside the museum's tank of glass;
And somehow quite unlike our Latin class
Sepias of the site,

Discoursed upon by Mr. Fish
In the familiar, rumpled suit,
Who tried to teach us the Ablative Absolute
And go part of his wish,

But a small part, and never traveled
On anything but the B.M.T.
Until the day of his death, when he would be,
At length, utterly graveled.

Anthony Hecht, 1972

Photograph: Roy Gumpel. *Vatican Staircase*, Rome, 1983

JOURNAL OF A VISIT TO EUROPE AND THE LEVANT

Thursday Feb 26: To Tortoni's, banker, to find out about S. Shaw or letters. Learnt nothing. To Capitol & Coliseum—Coliseum like great hollow among hills. Hopper of Greylock. Slope of concentric ruins overgrown. Mountainous. Museum of Capitol. Hall of Emperors. "That Tiberius? he don't look so bad at all"—It was he. A look of sickly evil,—intellect without manliness and sadness without goodness. Great brain overrefinements. Solitude—Dying Gladiator. Shows that humanity existed amid the barbarians of the Roman time, as it [does] now among Christian barbarians. Antinous, beautiful.—Walked to the Pincian hill—gardens and statuary—overlooking Piazza del Populo.— Fashion and Rank—Preposterous (pouting? posturing? twisting?) within stone's throw of Antinous. How little influence has truth on the world!—Fashion everywhere ridiculous, but most so in Rome. No place where lonely man will feel more lonely than in Rome (or Jerusalem). Fine view of St. Peter's from Pincian.—In the evening walked to Cafe Greco in Via Condotti. "English sculptor" with dirty hands &c. Dense smoke. Rowdy looking chaps &c.— Home and to bed. (Stopped at evening in picture dealers; offered a Cenci for $4. Surprisingly cheap.) Fine lounge in Piazza di Espagna among picture and curity [curiosity] dealers, and in Via Condotti, also.

Friday Feb 27: Tried to find A[merican?] Consul, Page, and Jarves. Failed in all.—Went to the Baths of Caracalla.—Wonderful. Massive. Ruins form, as it were, natural bridges of thousands of arches. There are glades, and thickets among the ruins—high up.—Thought of Shelley. Truly, he got his inspiration here. Corresponds with his drama and mind. Still majestic, and desolate [grandeurs].—After much troubles and sore travel without a guide managed to get to Protestant Burial Ground and pyramid of Cestius under walls. Read Keats' epitaph. Separated from the adjacent ground by trench.— Shelley in other ground. Plain stone.—(Went from Caracalla to Shelley's grave by natural process.) Thence to Cenci Palace, by way of Suspension Bridge, Isle of Tiber, theater of Marcellus (blacksmiths shops &c. in arches—black with centuries grime and soot—built upon above and inhabited)—Orsini Palace and Ghetto. Tragic looking place enough. The big sloping arch.—Part of it inhabited, part desolate.—Thence to Farnese palace—finest architecture of all the palaces (private). Farnese Hercules and Farnese Toro formerly here. Now in Museum Borbonco, Naples. Thence to St. Angelo Bridge and St. Peter's. And to dinner and bed.—Remarked the banks of Tiber near St. Angelo— fresh, alluvial look near masonry—primeval as Ohio in the midst of all these monuments of the centuries.

Herman Melville, 1857

Photograph: Everett McCourt. *Ponte Sant'Angelo, Rome,* 1978

ITALIAN BACKGROUNDS

As with the study of Italian pictures, so it is with Italy herself. The country is divided not in *partes tres*, but in two: a foreground and a background. The foreground is the property of the guide-book and of its product, the mechanical sight-seer; the background, that of the dawdler, the dreamer and the serious student of Italy. This distinction does not imply any depreciation of the foreground. It must be known thoroughly before the middle distance can be enjoyed: there is no short cut to an intimacy with Italy. Nor must the analogy of the devotional picture be pushed too far. The famous paintings, statues, and buildings of Italy are obviously the embodiment of its historic and artistic growth; but they have become slightly conventionalized by being too long used as the terms in which Italy is defined. They have stiffened into symbols, and the life of which they were once the most complete expression has evaporated in the desiccating museum-atmosphere to which their fame has condemned them. To enjoy them, one must let in on them the open air of an observation detached from tradition. Since they cannot be evaded they must be deconventionalized; and to effect this they must be considered in relation to the life of which they are merely the ornamental facade.

Edith Wharton, 1907

Photographs: Ruth Thorne-Thomsen.
Views from the Shoreline: Venice and *Harlequin Head*, 1986

THE COLISEUM

But stay! these walls—these ivy-clad arcades—
These mouldering plinths—these sad and blackened
   shafts—
These vague entablatures—this crumbling frieze—
These shattered cornices—this wreck—this ruin—
These stones—alas! these gray stones—are they all—
All of the famed, and the colossal left
By the corrosive Hours to Fate and Me?

Edgar Allan Poe, ca. 1830

Photograph: Aaron Siskind, *Arch of Constantine*, Rome, 1963

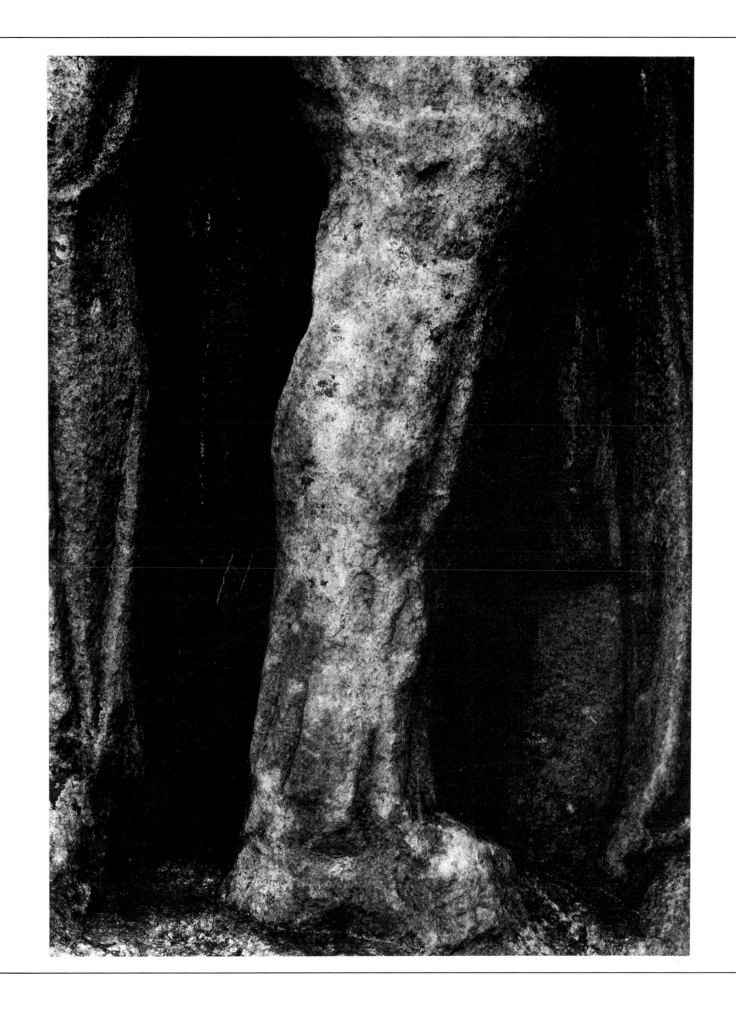

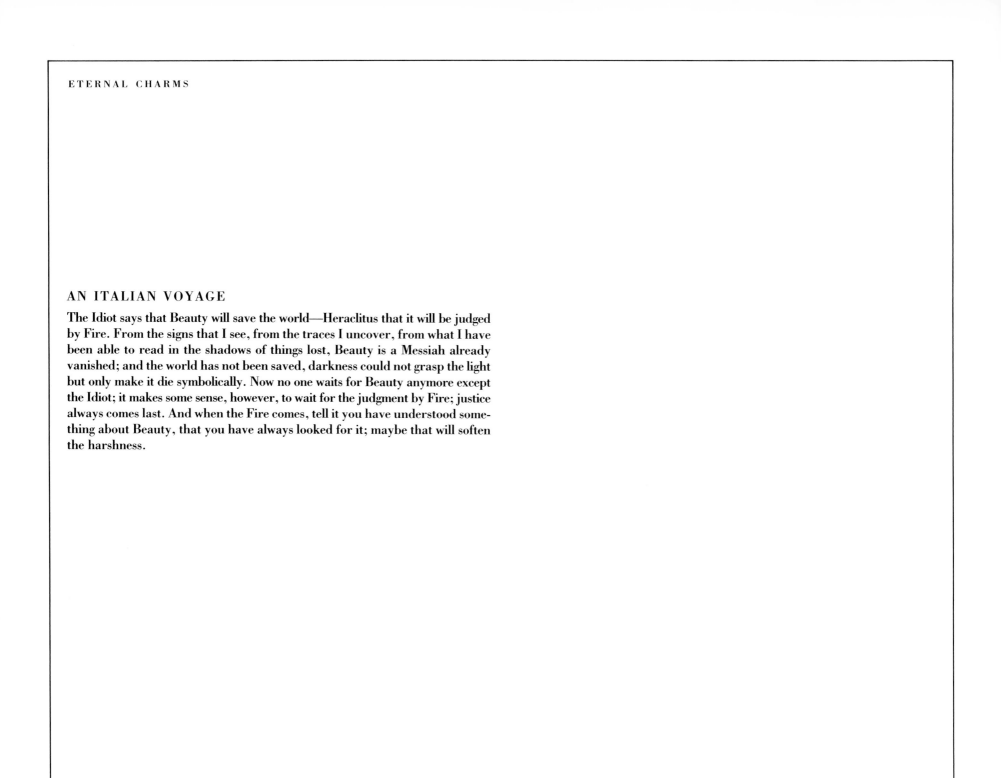

AN ITALIAN VOYAGE

The Idiot says that Beauty will save the world—Heraclitus that it will be judged by Fire. From the signs that I see, from the traces I uncover, from what I have been able to read in the shadows of things lost, Beauty is a Messiah already vanished; and the world has not been saved, darkness could not grasp the light but only make it die symbolically. Now no one waits for Beauty anymore except the Idiot; it makes some sense, however, to wait for the judgment by Fire; justice always comes last. And when the Fire comes, tell it you have understood something about Beauty, that you have always looked for it; maybe that will soften the harshness.

Guido Ceronetti, 1983

Photograph: Marcia Lippman. *Venice Trilogy, III*, 1987

LETTER TO WILLIAM DUNLAP

Dr. [G] Parkman, during my sophomore year, proposed to assist me in obtaining some knowledge of anatomy. He supplied me with bones, preparations, &c. every week; as also with such books as I could not get from the college library. He not only continued this kindness during the three years of my remaining college life, but lent me generous assistance in forwarding my studies by travel. I began to *study* art in Rome, in 1826. Until then I had rather amused myself with clay and marble than studied. When I say, that those materials were familiar to my touch, I say all that I profited by my boyish efforts. They were rude. I lived with poets and poetry, and could not than see that my art was to be studied from folk who eat their three meals every day. I *gazed* at the Apollo and the Venus, and *learned* very little by it. It was not till I ran through all the galleries and studios of Rome, and had had under my eye the genial forms of Italy that I began to feel nature's value. I had before adored her, but as a Persian does the sun, with my face to the earth. I then began to examine her—and entered on that course of study in which I am still toiling.

Horatio Greenough, December 1, 1833

Photograph: Aaron Siskind. *Appia Antica, No. 7*, Rome, 1963

IN SICILY

"Yes," said I, "I knew how a woman's formed better than ever, at seven."

"Better than ever?" said my mother.

"Better than ever," said I. "I knew it, I saw it. I had it always before my eyes, how a woman's formed."

"What d'you mean?" my mother exclaimed. "You used to think about it?"

"No," said I. "I didn't think about it. I knew it and saw it. That was all. Enough isn't it?"

"Whose did you see?" my mother asked.

"Every woman's . . . It was very natural to me. It wasn't cunning."

So it was. It was not cunning. Indeed, it was Woman I saw! At seven one does not know the evils of the world, nor grief and hopelessness; one is not possessed by abstract furies; but one knows woman. Never does a male know woman better than at the age of seven or less. Then she appears before him not as solace, not as delight, not even as a plaything. She is the certainty of the world, immortal.

Elio Vittorini, 1949

Photograph: Mimmo Jodice. *Centocamerelle*, Naples, 1982

SOUR LIFE

"Period. New paragraph?"

"No, no, same paragraph. And you? So tell me, how was the first time for you?"

"Come on, dictate."

"No, really. What was it like for you?"

"God, who can remember?"

"You really can't recall a single detail?"

"No. Can you?"

"Yeah, I can."

"So, how was it?"

Luciano Bianciardi, 1978

Photograph: David Hyman. *Autumn in Italy*, 1982

LETTER TO AUSTIN BRYANT

Dear Brother,

Some letters of mine which have been published in the *Evening Post* have probably informed you where I am as well as made you acquainted with the principal incidents of my journey. A few days since I received mother's letter of the 3d of January which reached me *in about* six weeks from the date. What it says of the snow and cold weather made me reflect on the difference between this climate and that I have left. We have seen no snow here except on the summits of the Apennines which have several times been seen brilliantly white with it beyond the green fields. The daisy has been in blossom all winter; the flowers of the crocus began to open in January, and about a week since cowslips, violets, and other flowers began to appear. This week peach and plum trees are in blossom. I have said the fields were green—but it is not with grass, for there is scarce any pasturage here—but with crops of wheat, turnips, cabbages, artichokes, the cauliflower, a kind of bean plant, and even flax. These plants, with the exception perhaps of the turnips and cabbages, grow very little it is true during the winter, but they keep healthy and advance somewhat, notwithstanding that the night frosts are frequently strong enough to cover still water with a thin crust of ice, which is, however, melted at noon. Orange and lemon trees grow here in the gardens in the open air; they do not blossom during the winter, but they are still hanging with fruit. Notwithstanding this mildness of the climate, the trees of deciduous foliage have remained as bare as in New England, and even now are so torpid to the influence of the sun and genial weather that there is little swelling of the buds to be perceived. There are several kinds of evergreens here, a kind of pine with a top like an umbrella, the ilex which is a species of oak with an abundance of spear-shaped leaves of the size of those of the plum tree, the olive with a grayish green leaf, and the cypress with a spiry growth like that of the Lombardy poplar but foliage like that of the red cedar. Then there are various evergreen shrubs, which are quite common, such as the laurel and the myrtle; even the blackberry bush is an evergreen here.

William Cullen Bryant, Pisa, Tuscany, February 24, 1835

Photograph: Giovanna dal Magro. *Found in Volterra*, 1984

LETTER TO ALICE JAMES

This is the place for history. I don't see how, if one lived here, historical problems could help being the most urgent ones for the mind. It would suit you admirably. Even art comes before one here much more as a problem—how to account for its development and decline—than as a refreshment and an edification. I really think that end is better served by the stray photographs which enter our houses at home, finding us in the midst of our work and surprising us.

William James, Florence, November 23, 1873

TRAVELS IN ITALY

Milan has often been called a functional city, demolished and rebuilt according to the need of the moment. It never managed to get old. It is true that each historical period left its ugly mark on Milan. The monarchy gave us the Piazza del Duomo, once described as a "monumental choreography in the banking style." Later, with a destructiveness that had no regard for the past, with its pomposity, its useless marble arches, the Fascist style replaced the banking style. Later still came a utopian Americanism, more American than America itself, with its skyscrapers and mechanical toys. Yet Milan is beautiful. . . . In Milan, one can escape from the frozen beauty of other Italian cities, which is often a limitation, a prison for those who dwell in them; one can escape from that unalterable perfection that sometimes leads to sterility. Here in Milan, beauty is a stimulus; here I find the freedom to live, to create, to engage in an unfinished project.

Guido Piovene, 1957

Photograph: Giovanni Ziliani and Paolo Giordano. *Milan*, 1983

A HILL

In Italy, where this sort of thing can occur,
I had a vision once—though you understand
It was nothing at all like Dante's, or the visions of saints,
And perhaps not a vision at all. I was with some friends,
Picking my way through a warm sunlit piazza
In the early morning. A clear fretwork of shadows
From huge umbrellas littered the pavement and made
A sort of lucent shallows in which was moored
A small navy of carts. Books, coins, old maps,
Cheap landscapes and ugly religious prints
Were all on sale. The colors and noise
Like the flying hands were gestures of exultation,
So that even the bargaining
Rose to the ear like a voluble godliness
And then, when it happened, the noises suddenly stopped,
And it got darker; pushcarts and people dissolved
And even the great Farnese Palace itself
Was gone, for all its marble; in its place
Was a hill, mole-colored and bare. It was very cold,
Close to freezing, with a promise of snow.
The trees were like old ironwork gathered for scrap
Outside a factory wall. There was no wind,
And the only sound for a while was the little click
Of ice as it broke in the mud under my feet.
I saw a piece of ribbon snagged on a hedge,
But no other sign of life. And then I heard
What seemed the crack of a rifle. A hunter, I guessed;
At least I was not alone. But just after that
Came the soft and papery crash
Of a great branch somewhere unseen falling to earth.

And that was all, except for the cold and silence
That promised to last forever, like the hill.

Then prices came through and fingers, and I was restored
To the sunlight and my friends. But for more than a week

I was scared by the plain bitterness of what I had seen.
All this happened about ten years ago,
And it hasn't troubled me since, but at last, today,
I remembered that hill; it lies just to the left
Of the road north of Poughkeepsie; and as a boy
I stood before it for hours in wintertime.

Anthony Hecht, 1968

Photograph: Emmet Gowin. *Garden*, Siena, 1979

SOURCE NOTES

Grateful acknowledgment is made to the authors and publishers named in these notes for permission to reproduce copyrighted material on the pages indicated at left.

18 Giorgio Manganelli. *Lunario dell'orfano sannita*. Turin: Einaudi, 1973.

20 T. S. Eliot. "The Waste Land," in *Collected Poems 1909–1962*, by T. S. Eliot, Copyright © 1936 by Harcourt Brace Jovanovich. Copyright © 1963, 1964, by T. S. Eliot. Reprinted by permission of the publisher.

22 Nathaniel Hawthorne. *Notes of Travel*. Cambridge, Massachusetts: Riverside Books, 1889.

24 From *Life, Letters, and Journals of George Ticknor*, vol. 2. Boston: James R. Osgood and Co., 1876.

26 Richard Wilbur. *Things of This World*. New York: Harcourt, Brace and Co., 1956.

28 Benjamin West, in *Letters and Papers of John Singleton Copley and Henry Pelham, 1739–1776*. Boston: The Massachusetts Historical Society, 1914.

30 Riccardo Bacchelli. *Italia per terra e per mare*. Milan: Mondadori, 1962.

32 Nathaniel Hawthorne. *Notes of Travel*. Cambridge, Massachusetts: Riverside Books, 1889.

34 Italo Calvino. *Invisible Cities*, translated by William Weaver. New York: Harcourt Brace Jovanovich, 1974. Reprinted by permission.

36 William Wetmore Story. *Roba di Roma*. Boston and New York: Houghton, Mifflin and Co., 1899.

38 Giuseppe Prezzolini. *The Legacy of Italy*. New York: S. F. Vanni, 1948. Reprinted by permission of S. F. Vanni.

38 Henry James. *Italian Hours*. New York: Houghton, Mifflin and Co., 1909.

40 Joel Tyler Headley. *Italy and the Italians in a Series of Letters*. New York: I. S. Platt, 1844.

42 John Cheever. "The Bella Lingua," in *The Brigadier and the Golf Widow*. New York: Harper and Row, 1964. Reprinted by permission of International Creative Management. Copyright © 1964 by John Cheever.

44 Carlo Sforza. *The Real Italians*. New York: Columbia University Press, 1942.

46 From *The Life and Letters of Christopher Pearse Cranch by His Daughter, Leonora Cranch Scott*. New York: AMS Press, 1969, reprinted from the edition of 1917, Boston and New York.

46 Alfredo Giuliani. "Way Back There the Void," 1988. Previously unpublished.

50 Alberto Arbasino. *Fratelli d'Italia*. Milan: Feltrinelli, 1967.

52 Henry Wadsworth Longfellow. *The Poetical Works*. New York: Houghton, Mifflin and Co., 1876.

54 William Dean Howells. *Italian Journeys*. New York: Houghton, Mifflin and Co., 1872.

56 Henry James. *Portraits of Places*, 1883. Reprinted New York: Leon Publishers, 1948.

58 Gertrude Stein. From *Italians in Geography and Plays*, 1922. Reprinted by permission of the Collection of American Literature, Beinecke Rare Book and Manuscript Library, Yale University, New Haven, Connecticut.

60 Giuseppe Prezzolini. *The Legacy of Italy*. New York: S. F. Vanni, 1948. Reprinted by permission of S. F. Vanni.

62 George Santayana. *My Host the World*, vol. 3. New York: Charles Scribner's Sons, 1953.

64 Ezra Pound. *The Cantos*. New York: New Directions, 1948.

66 Mark Twain, *The Innocents Abroad, or, The New Pilgrim's Progress; Being Some Account of the Steamship Quaker City's Pleasure Excursion to Europe and the Holy Land*, 1869. Reprinted New York: Viking Press, The Library of America, 1984.

68 Alberto Arbasino. *Fratelli d'Italia*. Milan: Feltrinelli, 1967.

70 Edmondo de Amicis. *Cuore: An Italian Schoolboy's Journal*, 1887. Published in translation New York: T. Y. Crowell and Company, 1895.

72 Carmelo Bene. *Nostra Signora dei Turchi*. Milan: Sugarco, 1978.

74 Aldo Palazzeschi. *Roma*. Florence: Vallecchi, 1925.

76 Ralph Waldo Emerson. *Journals*, vol. 3. Boston and New York: Houghton, Mifflin and Co., 1909–1914.

78 Umberto Eco. *Il Costume di casa*. Milan: Bompiani, 1973.

80 From *Letters of Charles Eliot Norton, with Biographical Comment by His Daughter Sara Norton and M. A. De Wolfe*. Boston and New York: Houghton, Mifflin and Co., 1913.

82 From *Letters and Papers of John Singleton Copley and Henry Pelham 1739–1776*. Boston: The Massachusetts Historical Society, 1914.

84 Washington Irving. *Notes and Journal of Travel in Europe, 1804–1805*, vol. 2. New York: Grolier Club, 1920.

88 Eugenio Montale. "Non c'e morte," in *L'Opera in versi*. Turin: Einaudi, 1980.

90 Antonio Gramsci. *Gli Intellettuali e l'organizzazione della cultura*. Turin: Einaudi, 1949 and 1968.

92 Pier Paolo Pasolini. *The Ashes of Gramsci*, translated by Norman Mac-Afee with Luciano Martinengo. New York: Random House, 1982. Milan: Garzanti, 1976.

94 Bartolo Cattafi. *The Dry Air of the Fire: Selected Poems*, translated by Ruth Feldman and Brian Swann. Ann Arbor, Michigan: Translation Press, 1981.

96 Ennio Flaiano. *Diario notturno e altri scritti*. Milan: Bompiani, 1956.

98 Luigi Barzini. *L'Antropometro Italiano*. Milan: Mondadori, 1973.

100 Giovanni Testori. *La Gilda del MacMahon*. Milan: Rizzoli, 1975.

102 Ann Cornelisen. *Women of the Shadows*. Boston and Toronto: Atlantic Monthly Press Book, Little, Brown and Company, 1976.

104 Elsa Morante. *Arturo's Island*, translated by Isabel Quigley. New York: Alfred A. Knopf. *L'Isola di Arturo*. Turin: Einaudi, 1952.

106 Eliot Ness, Jr. Unpublished manuscript, 1988.

108 Umberto Saba. *Il Canzoniere*. Turin: Einaudi, 1948.

110 Rocco Scottelaro. *L'Uva puttanella*. Bari: Laterza, 1975. First edition 1956, with preface by Carlo Levi.

112 Ezra Pound. *The Cantos of Ezra Pound*. New York: New Directions, 1969. Reprinted by permission.

114 Truman Capote. *The Dogs Bark: Public People and Private Places*. New York: Random House, Inc., 1973. Copyright © 1973 by Truman Capote. Reprinted by permission of Random House, Inc.

116 Margaret Fuller Ossoli. *At Home and Abroad*, edited by Arthur B. Fuller, 1856. Reprinted Port Washington, New York, and London: Kennikat Press, 1971.

118 Ernest Hemingway. *Across the River and into the Trees* New York: Charles Scribner and Sons, 1950. Reprinted by permission of Charles Scribner's Sons, an imprint of Macmillan Publishing Company. Copyright © 1950 by Ernest Hemingway. Copyright renewed 1978 by Mary Hemingway.

120 Luigi Malerba *Diario di un sognatore*. Turin: Einaudi, 1981.

122 Giorgio Manganelli. *Agli dei Ulteriori*. Turin: Einaudi, 1972.

126 Natalia Ginzburg. *Mai devi domandarmi*. Milan: Garzanti, 1976.

128 Amelia Rosselli. *Documenti, 1966–1973*. Milan: Garzanti, 1976.

130–135 Alberto Savinio. *Torre di guardia*. Palermo: Sellerio Editore, 1977.

132 Bernard Malamud. "Life Is Better Than Death," in *Idiots First*. New York: Farrar, Straus and Giroux, 1963.

136 Vitaliano Brancati. *I Piaceri*. Milan: Bompiani, 1974.

138 Henry T. Tuckerman. *Italian Sketch Book*. New York: J. C. Ricker, 1848.

140 Ann Cornelisen. *Torregreca*. Boston and Toronto: Little, Brown and Company, 1969. Reprinted by permission of the Wallace Literary Agency, Inc. Copyright © 1969 by Ann Cornelisen.

142 Ennio Flaiano. *Diario notturno e altri scritti*. Milan: Bompiani, 1956.

144 Edmund Wilson. *Europe without Baedeker*. New York: Farrar, Straus and Giroux, 1966.

146 Carlo Emilio Gadda. *That Awful Mess on Via Merulana*, translated by William Weaver. New York: George Braziller, 1965. *Quer pasticciaccio brutto de Via Merulana*. Milan: Garzanti, 1957.

148 James Fenimore Cooper. *Gleanings in Europe: Italy*, 1838. Reprinted Albany: State University of New York Press, 1981.

150–155 From *Opera Omnia di Benito Mussolini*, vol. 21. Florence: La Fenice, 1956.

154 Henry James. *Transatlantic Sketches*. Boston: James R. Osgood and Company, 1876.

156 James Sloan. *Rambles in Italy*. Baltimore: N. G. Maxwell, 1818.

158 Henry Wadsworth Longfellow. *The Poetical Works of Henry Wadsworth Longfellow*. Boston and New York: Houghton, Mifflin and Co., 1889, 1891.

160 Matilde Serao. *Il ventre di Napoli*. Naples: Francesco Perrella, 1906.

164 Mark Twain. *The Innocents Abroad; or, The New Pilgrim's Progress; Being Some Account of the Steamship Quaker City's Pleasure Excursion to Europe and the Holy Land*, 1869. Reprinted New York: Viking Press, The Library of America, 1984.

166 Rembrandt Peale. *Notes on Italy*. Philadelphia: Carey, 1831.

168 Corrado Alvaro. *Itinerario italiano*. Milan: Bompiani, 1941.

170 Herman Melville. *Journal of a Visit to Europe and the Levant, 1856–1857*, edited by Howard C. Horsford. Princeton, New Jersey: Princeton University Press, 1955.

172 Nathaniel Hawthorne. *Notes of Travel*. Cambridge, Massachusetts: Riverside Books, 1889.

174 Morris West. *The Salamander*. New York: William Morrow and Co., 1973.

176 James Fenimore Cooper. *Gleanings in Europe, Italy*, 1838. Reprinted Albany: State University of New York Press, 1981.

178 J. W. De Forest. *European Acquaintance*. New York: Harper and Brothers, Publisher, 1858.

180–183 Italo Calvino. *Italian Folktales*, translated by George Martin. New York and London: Harcourt, Brace, Jovanovich, 1980.

184 Mary McCarthy. *The Stones of Florence*. New York: Harcourt, Brace and Co., 1959.

186 Benedetto Croce. *The Aesthetic as the Science of Expression and General Linguistics*, translated by Douglas Ainslie. London: Macmillan and Co., 1909.

188 Ennio Flaiano. *Diario notturno e altri scritti*. Milan: Bompiani, 1956.

190 Riccardo Bacchelli. *Italia per terra e per mare*, vol. 20 in *Tutte le opere*. Milan: Mondadori, 1962.

192 Bernard Berenson. *The Passionate Sightseer: From the Diaries 1947 to 1956*. New York: Simon and Schuster, 1960. Reprinted by permission of Thames and Hudson Ltd, London, Copyright © 1960.

194 Henry James. *W. W. Story and His Friends*. Boston: Houghton, Mifflin and Co., 1903.

198 Eugenio Montale. *L'Opera in versi*. Turin: Einaudi, 1980.

200 James Russell Lowell. *Fireside Travels*. Boston: Houghton, Mifflin and Co., 1894.

202 Mary McCarthy: *The Stones of Florence*. New York: Harcourt, Brace and Co. 1959.

204–207 Henry Adams. *The Education of Henry Adams*. Boston: Houghton, Mifflin and Co., 1916.

208 Riccardo Bacchelli. *Italia per terra e per mare*, vol. 20 in *Tutte le opere*. Milan: Mondadori, 1962.

210 From "To an Old Philosopher in Rome," in *The Collected Poems of Wallace Stevens*. New York: Random House, 1952. Copyright © 1952 by Wallace Stevens. Reprinted by permission of Alfred A. Knopf, Inc.

212 Robert Lowell. "Beyond the Alps," from *Life Studies*. New York: Farrar, Straus, Giroux, 1967.

214 Anthony Hecht. "Rome," from *Millions of Strange Shadows*. New York: Atheneum, 1977. Reprinted by permission of Atheneum Publishers, an imprint of Macmillan Publishing Company. Copyright © 1977 by Anthony E. Hecht.

216 Herman Melville. *Journal of a Visit to Europe and the Levant, 1856–1857*, edited by Howard C. Horsford. Princeton, New Jersey: Princeton University Press, 1955.

218 Edith Wharton. *Italian Backgrounds*. New York: Charles Scribner's Sons, 1907.

220 Edgar Allan Poe. "The Coliseum," in *Poe: Poetry and Tales*. New York: Viking Press, The Library of America, 1975.

222 Guido Ceronetti. "L'Idiota dice che la Bellezza," in *Un Viaggio in Italia*. Turin: Einaudi, 1983.

224 From *Letters of Horatio Greenough, American Sculptor*, edited by Nathalia Wright. Madison: The University of Wisconsin Press, 1972.

226 Elio Vittorini. *In Sicily*, translated by Wilfred David. New York: New Directions, 1949. First edition, published 1942.

228 Luciano Bianciardi. *La Vita agra*. Milan: Rizzoli, 1978.

230 William Cullen Bryant II and Thomas G. Voss, eds. *The Letters of William Cullen Bryant*, vol. 1. New York: Fordham University Press, 1975.

232 From *Letters of William James*. Boston: Little, Brown and Company, 1926.

232 Guido Piovene. *Viaggio in Italia*. Milan: Mondadori, 1957.

234 Anthony Hecht. "A Hill," from *The Hard Hours*. New York: Atheneum, 1968. Reprinted by permission of Atheneum Publishers, an imprint of Macmillan Publishing Company. Copyright © 1964 by Anthony E. Hecht. Originally published in *The New Yorker*.

INDEX OF WRITERS AND PHOTOGRAPHERS